DIABETIC AIR FRYER COOKBOOK FOR BEGINNERS

1200 Days Delicious Air Fryer Recipes for Prediabetes, Diabetes, and Type 2 Diabetes Newly Diagnosed

Copyright©2023 Elizabeth White
All rights reserved. No part of this book may be reproduced
or used in any manner without the prior written permission
of the copyright owner, except for the use of brief quotations
in a book review.
Printed by Amazon in the USA.

Disclaimer : Although the author and publisher have made every effort to ensure that the information in this book was correct at press time, the author and publisher do not assume and hereby disclaim any liability to any party for any loss, damage, or disruption caused by errors or omissions, whether such errors or omissions result from negligence, accident, or any other cause. this book is not intended as a substitute for the medical advice of physicians.

TABLE OF CONTENTS

INTRODUCTION ... 7

DESSERTS RECIPES ... 8

Keto Air Fryer Churro Sticks ... 8

Strawberry Banana "ice Cream" ... 8

Apple Walnut French Toast ... 9

Everything Bagel Cheese Ball ... 9

4-ingredient Peanut Butter Cookies ... 9

Cool Weather Cobbler ... 10

Sugar Free Low Carb Peanut Butter Cookies ... 10

Grilled Peaches With Walnuts ... 11

Mini Apple Chimichanga ... 11

Keto Flourless Chocolate Brownies ... 12

Fried Cheesecake Bites ... 12

Greek Yogurt Chocolate Mousse ... 13

Milk Chocolate Peanut Butter Banana Smoothie ... 13

Chocolate Peanut Butter Chia Seed Pudding ... 13

5 Ingredient Blueberry Protein Muffins ... 14

Blueberry Almond Pancakes ... 14

Keto Chocolate Cake Recipe ... 15

Almond, Wild Blueberry, And Flax Smoothie ... 15

Instant Pot Chia Berry Crepes ... 15

No-bake Peanut Butter & Chocolate Bites ... 16

Chocolate Walnut Mug Cake ... 16

Air Fryer Keto Blueberry Muffins ... 17

Fruit And Almond Smoothie ... 17

Easiest Low Carb Blondie Mug Cake With Prune Glaze ... 17

Peppermint Chocolate "nice Cream" ... 18

Instant Pot Almond-toffee Topped Pears ... 18

Strawberry-lemon Cheesecake ... 19

Carrot Cake Whoopie Pies ... 19

Banana Chocolate "ice Cream" ... 20

VEGETABLES RECIPES ... 21

Keto Air Fryer Zucchini Fries ... 21

Instant Pot Vegetarian Thai Mushroom Soup ... 21

Lentil Chili ... 22

Air-fryer Zucchini ... 22

Bacon-wrapped Asparagus In The Air Fryer ... 23

Slow-cooker Spinach Artichoke Dip ... 23

Vegetarian Sliders With Black Beans, Chard & Poblanos ... 23

Ham And Broccoli Frittata 24

Vegetarian Antipasto Sliders 25

Air-fryer Fried Green Tomatoes 25

Air Fried Cabbage 26

Keto Vegetarian Lasagna 26

Sweet Potato Hash Stuffed Portobello Mushrooms 27

Broccoli Onion Latkes 28

Vegan Cauliflower Buffalo Wings 28

Creamy Cauliflower-jalapeño Popper Dip 29

Cheesy Black Bean & Corn-stuffed Portobello Mushrooms 29

Low Carb Veggie Fried Rice Bowl 30

Bolognese Zucchini Boats In The Air Fryer 31

Air-fryer Red Potatoes 31

Air-fryer Zucchini Fritters 31

Air-fryer Asparagus 32

Air Fryer Sweet Potato Nachos 32

Crispy Air Fryer Broccoli Bites With Nutritional Yeast 33

FISH AND SEAFOOD RECIPES 34

Air-fryer Bacon-wrapped Scallops 34

Tuna Ceviche 34

Air-fryer Crab Cakes 34

Air-fryer Pistachio-crusted Sea Bass 35

Air-fryer Tilapia 36

Air Fryer Keto Coconut Shrimp 36

Air-fryer Popcorn Shrimp 37

Air-fryer Tuna Steak 37

Air Fryer Coconut Shrimp 38

Air Fryer Scallops Recipe 38

Honey Soy-glazed Salmon 38

Perfect Air Fryr Salmon Fillets 39

Air-fryer Tuna Patties 39

Air-fryer Beer-battered Fish 40

Air-fryer Scallops 41

Air-fryer Coconut Shrimp 41

Crab Stuffed Shrimp 42

Asian Tuna Salad 43

Air-fryer Salmon With Horseradish Rub 43

Instant Pot Panko-crusted Cod 44

Fried Shrimp 44

Air Fryer Shrimp Recipe 45

Teriyaki Salmon Air Fryer 45

Air-fryer Fish Tacos 46

Air-fryer Shrimp 47

Air-fryer Salmon Cakes 47

Air-fryer Fish Cakes 47

Air-fryer Salmon 48

BEEF, PORK AND LAMB RECIPES ... 49

Classic Beef Stew ... 49

Tuscan-spiced Pork & Mashed Potatoes With Green Beans And Roasted Tomato Dressing ... 49

Air-fryer Pork Chops ... 50

Air-fryer Pork Tenderloin ... 51

Air Fryer Steak ... 51

Bulgogi ... 52

Air-fryer Steak Fajitas ... 52

Air Fryer Jalepeno Poppers ... 53

Ham And Edamame Chop Salad ... 53

Beef Fajitas ... 54

Asian Pork Chops ... 54

Air-fryer Meatloaf ... 55

Air-fryer Empanadas ... 55

Beef Stroganoff ... 56

Jamaican Pork Tenderloin Roast ... 56

Air Fryer Instant Pot Vortex Pork Tenderloin ... 57

Air-fryer Meatballs ... 57

Airfryer Lemony Lamb Chops With Fennel & Olives ... 58

Signature Skillet Supper ... 58

Classic Meatloaf ... 59

Keto Pork Chops - Super Crispy! ... 60

Air Fryer Salt And Pepper Crispy Pork Belly Crack ... 60

Air Fryer Pork Chops ... 60

Chili-cheese Nachos ... 61

Pork Schnitzel With Creamy Dill Sauce ... 61

POULTRY RECIPES ... 63

Chicken And Cabbage ... 63

Baja Turkey Burgers ... 63

Bacon Wrapped Chicken Tenders ... 64

Curry Seasoned Chicken Drumsticks ... 64

Air-fryer Turkey Stuffed Peppers ... 65

Best Air Fryer Chicken Fajitas Recipe ... 65

Turkey Skillet Casserole ... 66

Sweet Chili Chicken, Sweet Potatoes, And Broccoli ... 66

Easy Keto Pizza Chicken Bake ... 67

Chicken Satay ... 68

Asian Chicken Salad ... 68

Instant Pot Chicken Sausage And Zucchini Stuffed Potatoes ... 69

Sheet Pan Chicken, Green Beans & Potatoes ... 69

Air-fryer Spinach & Feta Turkey Burgers ... 70

Air-fryer Turkey Breast ... 70

Air-fryer Chicken Cordon Bleu ... 71

Chicken Fried Rice 71

Crock Pot Moo Shu Chicken.. 72

Air-fryer Chicken Tenders... 72

Homemade AirFryer Sweet Potato Chicken Nuggets
.... 73

Greek Chicken Kabobs 74

Creamy Tomato Chicken 75

Instant Pot Freezer Fix Chili 75

Dijon Chicken W/ Zucchini & Tomatoes................. 76

Brochetas (pinchos) De Albóndigas 76

Easy Chicken Meatloaf 77

Baked Teriyaki Chicken... 77

Air-fryer Turkey Croquettes 78

Skillet Creamy Lemon Chicken With Cauliflower... 78

Extra Crispy Air Fryer Chicken Wings 79

OTHER FAVORITE RECIPES 80

Air Fryer Shishito Peppers With Lemon Aioli 80

4-layer Stuffed Avocado 80

Air-fryer French Toast Sticks 81

Brazilian Guacamole 81

Watermelon Gazpacho 82

Corn And Cheese Phyllo Empanadas...................... 82

Instant Pot Asian Spaghetti Squash 83

Japanese Cucumber Salad 84

Loaded Sheet-pan Nachos.. 84

Instant Pot Lentils And Poached Eggs 85

Sweet Potato-black Bean Burgers 85

Air-fryer Jalapeño Poppers 86

Butternut Squash Queso Fundido 86

Chunky Black Bean Salsa With Corn & Bell Pepper 87

Low Carb Baked Feta Rice.. 88

Garbanzo Bean And Arugula Salad 88

SNACKS, APPETIZERS AND SIDERS RECIPES... 89

Air-fryer Crispy Chickpeas 89

Air-fryer Cauliflower Gnocchi With Marinara
Dipping Sauce 89

Easiest Air Fryer Kale Chips.. 89

Double-tahini Hummus 90

Air-fryer Tofu Steaks 90

Crispy Garlic Keto Croutons Recipe Air Fryer 90

Air Fryer Pumpkin Seeds 91

Air Fryer Tofu 91

Avocado Fries With Sriracha Aioli 92

Perfectly Roasted Air Fryer Sweet Potato Chunks .. 92

Air-fryer Blooming Onions... 93

Sweet Potato Skins With Guacamole 93

Keto Fried Pickles.. 94

5

Garlic Parmesan Kale Chips 94

Better Mashed Potatoes 94

Roasted Buffalo Chickpeas 95

Air Fryer Crispy Bacon 95

Oven-fried Pickles 95

Make Egg Rolls In The Air Fryer For A High-fiber Appetizer That Everyone Will Love 96

Crispy Parmesan Mushroom Fries With Ranch Sauce 96

Air-fryer Potato Chips 97

Air Fryer Zucchini Fries - Keto 97

Cinnamon-sugar Roasted Chickpeas 97

Air-fryer Plantains 98

BREAKFAST RECIPES 99

Easy Egg Salad 99

Fast-fix Bean Burrito 99

Herbed Soft Scrambled Eggs On Toast 99

Cinnamon French Vanilla Overnight Oats 100

Guilt-free Breakfast Sausage Patties 100

Breakfast Quesadilla 100

Spinach And Parmesan Egg Bites 101

Oat Congee 101

Meat Lover's Breakfast Cups 102

Veggie Breakfast Wrap 102

Instant Pot Wheat Berry, Black Bean, And Avocado Salad 103

Breakfast Egg And Ham Burrito 103

Air Fryer Crisp Egg Cups 104

Lemon Chiffon With Fresh Berries 104

High-fiber Zucchini Muffins 104

Breaded Air-fryer Summer Squash 105

Crispy Air Fryer French Toast 105

Air-fryer Wasabi Egg Salad Wraps 106

Air Fryer Cheesy Baked Eggs 106

Air Fryer Scrambled Eggs 106

Bangers And Mash 107

Perfect & Easy To Peel Air Fryer Hard Boiled Eggs 107

Brown Rice Congee With Stir-fried Herbs 107

Prosciutto And Spinach Egg Cups 108

INTRODUCTION

When living with diabetes, cooking oftentimes can become an overwhelming and tedious task. You may find yourself spending hours in the kitchen preparing meals, which leaves you feeling drained, exhausted, and stressed out. As much as I love cooking, I don't enjoy spending my hours on overly complicated recipes in the kitchen. I prefer to keep things easy, simple, and full of flavor. When it comes to protein and vegetables, I have a difficult time coming up with fun and delicious ways to prepare them. In this blog post, we are going to take a look at easy ways to cook a variety of proteins and vegetables that only require the use of an air fryer.

WHY YOU SHOULD BUY AN AIR FRYER

My air fryer is hands down my most used kitchen gadget. Here are just some of the benefits to air frying food:

- **Reduction of Saturated Fat Intake:** When using an air fryer, you do not need to use as much saturated fat, like butter and oil, when cooking to make foods crispy and crunchy. High consumption of saturated fat intake has been linked to increased insulin resistance and impaired insulin sensitivity which can make blood sugars more difficult to manage for people with diabetes.

- **Convenience:** the concept of air frying is similar to convection cooking in that it uses forced, heated and circulated air to cook foods faster and evenly in the process. Air fryers can significantly cut down cooking time compared to using traditional gas or electric ovens.

- **Easy to Clean:** Since little to no oil is being used, there are no hard messes to clean up afterwards. The baskets inside air fryers are non-stick so it usually just requires a rinse after each use.

- **Versatility:** Most air fryers come with a cookbook along with instructions for use. Air fryers usually just require pressing a few buttons much like a microwave oven. There are many accessories for air fryers now that can allow you to cook anything and everything from hard boiled eggs to dessert to full course dinner!

IMPORTANCE OF PROTEIN & FIBER IN BLOOD SUGAR MANAGEMENT

Before diving into recipes, it is important to touch upon the importance of protein and fiber in regards to blood sugar management. We all know that carbohydrates raise blood sugar, but we sometimes forget to shift our focus to foods that can make your blood sugar management easier. In general, protein has a small effect on blood sugar levels and often tends to help stabilize blood sugar levels by slowing down the absorption of carbohydrates at a meal. Additionally, fiber helps support blood sugar management by slowing down the absorption of glucose from digesting carbohydrates. These two nutrients have a significant impact on blood sugar management and shouldn't be forgotten about either- nor does this mean that you need to eat plain, boring grilled chicken or steamed broccoli. You deserve to make these foods fun and flavorful while managing your blood sugars.

DESSERTS RECIPES

Keto Air Fryer Churro Sticks

Servings: 5
Cooking Time: 8-10 Minutes

Ingredients:
- 1 ½ C. Mozzarella cheese
- 2 oz. Cream cheese
- 1 C. Almond flour
- 2 Tbsp. Swerve confectioners sugar substitute
- ½ tsp. Cinnamon
- 1 ½ tsp. Baking powder
- 1 Egg
- 2 Tbsp. Heavy whipping cream
- For the topping:
- 1 Tbsp. Butter melted
- 2 Tbsp. Swerve granulated sweetener
- 1 tsp. Cinnamon

Directions:
1. Preheat the air fryer to 350 degrees.
2. In a microwave safe bowl, combine the mozzarella cheese and cream cheese. Heat for 30 seconds at a time until the cheeses are completely melted and well blended into a dough.
3. Knead the almond flour, baking powder, Swerve confectioners sugar substitute and ½ teaspoon of cinnamon into the melted cheese mixture. It is best to use your hands and be patient, as this can take a few minutes.
4. Blend the egg and heavy whipping cream into the dough mixture until smooth.
5. Spoon the dough into a piping bag or other tool with a large star shaped decorators tip on the end.
6. Place 3-4 inch long strips of the dough onto a parchment lined tray.
7. Cook the churro sticks in the air fryer for 4-5 minutes per side or until each side is browned and the churro sticks are cooked through.
8. Brush the air fried churro sticks with the melted butter.
9. Mix together the granulated sweetener and 1 teaspoon of cinnamon in a small bowl.
10. Sprinkle the cinnamon over the buttered churro sticks and serve.

Nutrition facts:
Calories Per Serving: 245; Total Fat: 21.6g; Sodium: 119mg; Total Carbs: 8.3g; Fiber: 2.6g; Sugars: 0.9g; Protein: 9.3g

Strawberry Banana "ice Cream"

Servings: 4

Ingredients:
- 2 bananas
- 1 cup sliced strawberries
- 2 tbsp coconut milk

Directions:
1. Peel bananas and slice into 1/4-inch rounds. Place in a bowl and freeze for at least 2 hours.
2. Once bananas are frozen, add them to a blender or food processor along with the strawberries and coconut milk. Blend on high speed 30 seconds. Scrape down the sides of the blender and blend on high 30 more seconds. Repeat this process until mixture is smooth and the texture of soft-serve ice cream. You can serve immediately or freeze for 30 minutes for a firmer texture.

Nutrition facts:

Calories Per Serving 80; Total Fat: 0g; Sodium: 0mg; Total Carbs: 19g; Fiber: 3g; Sugars: 10g; Protein:1g

Apple Walnut French Toast

Servings:4

Cooking Time: 10 Minutes

Ingredients:

- 2 tsp olive oil (or unsalted butter)
- 1 cup apple (diced)
- 1 cup egg substitute
- 1/4 tsp ground cinnamon (plus 1/2 tsp, divided)
- 1/4 tsp nutmeg
- 1 tsp sugar
- 8 Cloudbread (rounds)
- 2 oz walnuts
- 2 tbsp maple syrup

Directions:

1. Preheat a large non-stick skillet over medium heat. Add 1 tablespoon of butter, apples, and 1/2 tsp cinnamon. Cook, stirring often, until apples soften, 5–7 minutes. Transfer apples to a small bowl and cover with foil to keep warm. Wipe out the skillet with a paper towel and reserve for later.
2. In a medium bowl, whisk together the egg substitute, ½ tsp cinnamon, nutmeg, and sugar.
3. Return the skillet to medium heat. Add the rest of the butter and swirl to coat the bottom.
4. Dip the cloud bread rounds into the egg mixture, turning to coat both sides. Place in the skillet and cook for 2-3 minutes per side, until the rounds begin to brown.
5. Divide rounds between plates. Top with apples, walnuts, maple syrup, and a light dusting of powdered sugar, if desired.

Nutrition facts:

Calories Per Serving 290; Total Fat: 22g; Sodium: 280mg; Total Carbs: 13g; Fiber: 2g; Sugars: 9g; Protein: 12g

Everything Bagel Cheese Ball

Servings:12

Ingredients:

- 8 ounces reduced-fat cream cheese, softened
- 1 ½ cups shredded Cheddar cheese
- 4 tablespoons everything bagel seasoning, divided

Directions:

1. Stir cream cheese, Cheddar and 2 tablespoons seasoning together in a medium bowl.
2. Coat a large piece of plastic wrap with cooking spray. Scoop the cheese mixture onto it. Using the plastic wrap to help you, form the cheese mixture into a ball, then wrap completely in plastic. Refrigerate for at least 1 hour.
3. Just before serving, pour the remaining 2 tablespoons seasoning into a shallow dish. Roll the cheese ball in the seasoning, pressing to adhere.

Nutrition facts:

Calories Per Serving107; Total Fat: 8g; Sodium: 235mg; Total Carbs: 3g; Fiber: 0g; Sugars: 1g; Protein: 5g

4-ingredient Peanut Butter Cookies

Servings:20

Cooking Time: 10 Minutes

Ingredients:

- 1 cup peanut butter
- 1 cup Splenda® Granulated Sweetener
- 1 large egg (beaten)
- 1 tsp vanilla extract

Directions:

1. Preheat oven to 350°F. In a large bowl, mix together peanut butter, Splenda sweetener, egg, and vanilla extract. Chill mixture in the fridge for at least 10 minutes.
2. Portion mixture into 1 tablespoon balls and place on an ungreased sheet pan. Press lightly with the tines of a fork to create a crosshatch pattern and flatten each cookie slightly.
3. Bake for 8 minutes. Let cool on sheet pan at least 5 minutes before transferring to a wire rack to finish cooling.

Nutrition facts:

Calories Per Serving80; Total Fat: 7g; Sodium: 50mg; Total Carbs: 3g; Fiber: 1g; Sugars: 1g; Protein: 4g

Cool Weather Cobbler

Servings:18

Cooking Time: 45 Minutes

Ingredients:

- 6 medium pears or apples (peeled, cored, and sliced)
- 1 cup fresh or frozen cranberries and/or pitted cherries
- 1 tbsp arrowroot powder
- 1 tsp ground cinnamon
- 1 tsp fresh ginger (grated)
- 1 tsp orange zest (freshly grated)
- 1 cup almond flour
- 2 cup old-fashioned rolled oats (not quick cooking) (gluten-free)
- 1/2 cup whole wheat flour
- 1/4 cup pumpkin seeds (unsalted, toasted)
- 1/4 cup unsalted almonds (raw, sliced)
- 1 tsp ground cinnamon
- 1/4 tsp fine sea salt
- 2 tbsp melted coconut oil or canola oil
- 1 tbsp Extra Virgin Olive Oil
- 1/3 cup pure maple syrup (preferably grade B)

Directions:

1. Preheat the oven to 350°F.
2. To make the filling, toss together all the fruit, the arrowroot powder, cinnamon, ginger, and orange zest in a medium bowl. Spread the filling in the bottom of an 8 x 12-inch baking dish.
3. To make the topping, stir together the almond flour, oats, flour, pumpkin seeds, almonds, cinnamon, and salt in another medium bowl. Drizzle in the coconut oil, olive oil, and maple syrup and mix until evenly combined.
4. Crumble the topping over the filling and bake for 40 minutes, or until the topping is brown and the fruit is bubbling. Remove cobbler from the oven and set aside to cool for 10 minutes before serving.

Nutrition facts:

Calories Per Serving 190; Total Fat: 9g; Sodium: 35mg; Total Carbs: 26g; Fiber: 5g; Sugars: 10g; Protein: 5g

Sugar Free Low Carb Peanut Butter Cookies

Servings:8

Cooking Time: 9 Minutes

Ingredients:

- 1 egg beaten
- 1 cup sugar substitute we use sukrin
- 1 cup all natural peanut butter we used 100% peanuts
- 1 teaspoon liquid stevia drops

Directions:

1. Combine ingredients into a dough.
2. Form dough into 24 balls
3. On a cutting board or cookie sheet, press balls with a fork to create classic criss cross on top.

4. Place 6 cookies spread out into air fryer basket or if using the Foodi you can use the air crisp basket (or even a perforated pizza pan on a trivet). If using an oven, spread cookies out at least an inch a part on a cookie sheet. (If baking in oven, you can bake in batches as big as your cookie sheet will allow.
5. Air Crisp or Air Fry at 325 for 8-10 minutes. Or, bake in a pre-heated 325 oven for 8-10 minutes.
6. Allow cookies to cool for a minute or two before removing with a spatula and placing on a plate to finish cooling.
7. Finish baking the rest of the cookies in batches.

Nutrition facts:

Calories Per Serving: 198; Total Fat: 17g; Sodium: 8mg; Total Carbs: 7g; Fiber: 3g; Sugars: 2g; Protein: 9g

Grilled Peaches With Walnuts

Servings:6
Cooking Time: 8 Minutes

Ingredients:
- 3 ripe peaches
- 2 tablespoons maple syrup
- oil optional for grilling
- To serve
- 2 tablespoons chopped walnuts
- ice cream optional

Directions:
1. Preheat the grill to medium heat.
2. Slice the peaches in half and remove the pit.
3. Place the peaches flesh side down and grill for about 4 minutes.
4. Turn the peaches skin side down and then drizzle with maple syrup.
5. Grill for another 4-6 minutes until soft. Larger peaches may need a few more minutes.
6. Remove and serve with ice cream and chopped walnuts.
7. Air Fryer Instructions:
8. Preheat Air Fryer to 350F / 180C.
9. Slice the peaches in half and remove the pit.
10. Place the peaches in the air fryer skin side down and then drizzle with maple syrup.
11. Air fry for 8-12 minutes until soft. Larger peaches may need a few more minutes.
12. Remove and serve with ice cream and chopped walnuts.
13. Firmer peaches may need a bit longer.

Nutrition facts:

Calories Per Serving: 62; Total Fat: 3g; Sodium: 1mg; Total Carbs: 8g; Fiber: 1g; Sugars: 7g; Protein: 1g

Mini Apple Chimichanga

Servings:4
Cooking Time: 15 Minutes

Ingredients:
- 2 apple (cored and chopped)
- 3 tbsp zero-calorie granulated sweetener, such as splenda (divided use)
- 1/2 tsp ground cinnamon
- 1/4 cup water
- 4 8-inch whole wheat flour tortillas
- 1 nonstick cooking spray

Directions:
1. Preheat oven to 400 degrees F
2. In a medium-sized saucepan, combine apples, 2 tbsp Splenda, cinnamon, and water. Bring to a boil, and cook until apples are soft. Remove from heat. Cool to room temperature.
3. To build the chimichangas, pile 2 tsp apple filling on each tortilla and fold each end over the filling. Roll the tortillas up and secure each one with a toothpick. Lightly coat the tortillas with cooking

spray. Place folded tortillas seam side down on baking sheet. Sprinkle evenly with remaining granulated sweetener. Bake for 5 minutes, then turn over and bake 5 minutes more.
4. Remove chimichangas from the baking sheet and place on individual plates. If desired, garnish with a scoop of ice cream or a dollop of whipped cream.

Nutrition facts:

Calories Per Serving 219; Total Fat: 9g; Sodium: 200mg; Total Carbs: 28g; Fiber: 3g; Sugars: 2g; Protein: 7g

Keto Flourless Chocolate Brownies

Servings: 6
Cooking Time: 35 Minutes

Ingredients:
- 1/2 cup Sugar-Free Chocolate Chips
- 1/2 cup Butter
- 3 Eggs
- 1/4 cup Truvia or other sweetener
- 1 tsp Vanilla extract

Directions:
1. In a microwave safe bowl, melt butter and chocolate for about 1 minute. Remove and stir well. You really want to use the heat within the butter and chocolate to melt the rest of the clumps. If you microwave until it's all melted, you've overcooked the chocolate. So get a spoon and start stirring. Add 10 seconds if needed but stir well before you decide to do that.
2. In a bowl, add eggs, sweetener, and vanilla and blend until light and frothy.
3. Pour the melted butter and chocolate into the bowl in a slow stream and beat again until it is well-incorporated.
4. Pour the mixture into greased springform container or cake pan and bake at 350F for 30-35 minutes until a knife inserted in the center emerges clean.
5. Serve with whipped cream if desired

Nutrition facts:

Calories Per Serving: 224; Total Fat: 23g; Sodium: 0mg; Total Carbs: 3g; Fiber: 1g; Sugars: 0g; Protein: 4g

Fried Cheesecake Bites

Servings: 16

Ingredients:
- 8 ounces cream cheese
- 1/2 cup erythritol
- 4 Tablespoons heavy cream, divided
- 1/2 teaspoon vanilla extract
- 1/2 cup almond flour
- 2 Tablespoons erythritol

Directions:
1. Allow the cream cheese to sit on the counter for 20 minutes to soften.
2. Fit a stand mixer with paddle attachment.
3. Mix the softened cream cheese, 1/2 cup erithrytol, vanilla and heavy cream until smooth.
4. Scoop onto a parchment paper lined baking sheet.
5. Freeze for about 30 minutes, until firm.
6. Mix the almond flour with the 2 Tablespoons erythritol in a small mixing bowl.
7. Dip the frozen cheesecake bites into 2 Tablespoons cream, then roll into the almond flour mixture.

Nutrition facts:

Calories Per Serving: 80; Total Fat: 7g; Sodium: 50mg; Total Carbs: 2g; Fiber: 0g; Sugars: 1g; Protein: 2g

Greek Yogurt Chocolate Mousse

Servings:6

Ingredients:
- 6 mini Hershey's Sugar-Free Special Dark Chocolate bars (chopped)
- 2 cup Plain Nonfat Greek yogurt (non-fat)
- 2 tbsp honey or 4 packets artificial sweetener
- 1 tsp vanilla extract
- 1/4 cup skim milk
- 6 tbsp whipped topping (non-fat)
- 2 cup fresh raspberries

Directions:
1. Add the chopped chocolate to a microwave-safe bowl. Microwave the chocolate on high for 1 minute, then stir. If not completely melted, microwave for 30 more seconds, then stir until all chunks are melted. If it is still not melted, microwave another 30 seconds and continue to stir, just until the chunks in the chocolate are melted. Do not overcook.
2. In a medium mixing bowl, whip the Greek yogurt with an electric mixer until fluffy. Add the honey, vanilla, and milk, and beat some more, then add the chocolate, a small amount at a time, beating in between additions.
3. Once all of the chocolate is mixed into the yogurt, divide the mousse into 6 portions and top each portion with 1/3 cup raspberries and 1 tablespoon whipped topping

Nutrition facts:
Calories Per Serving 130; Total Fat: 4g; Sodium: 35mg; Total Carbs:17g; Fiber: 3g; Sugars: 11g; Protein: 9g

Milk Chocolate Peanut Butter Banana Smoothie

Servings:2

Ingredients:
- 1 (8-oz) bottle Splenda Diabetes Care Chocolate Shake
- 1/2 frozen banana
- 1 tbsp chia seeds
- 1 tbsp peanut butter
- 1 cup ice

Directions:
1. Place all ingredients in a blender. Blend until all ingredients are combined and smooth. Divide smoothie between two glasses and serve.

Nutrition facts:
Calories Per Serving 190; Total Fat: 11g; Sodium: 90mg; Total Carbs: 19g; Fiber: 7g; Sugars: 4g; Protein: 11g

Chocolate Peanut Butter Chia Seed Pudding

Servings:3

Ingredients:
- 2 tbsp unsweetened cocoa powder
- 2 tbsp Splenda or stevia
- 1/4 cup powdered peanut butter
- 1/4 cup chia seeds
- 1 cup skim milk or unsweetened almond milk
- 1 tsp vanilla extract

Directions:
1. Mix cocoa powder, Splenda or stevia, and powdered peanut butter together, and incorporate well so there are no lumps.
2. Stir in the chia seeds and stir well to combine.

3. Whisk in the milk and vanilla. Let sit for 5 minutes, then whisk again. Cover and refrigerate for at least 2 hours before serving.

Nutrition facts:

Calories Per Serving 150; Total Fat:7g; Sodium: 100mg; Total Carbs: 18g; Fiber: 8g; Sugars: 5g; Protein: 10g

5 Ingredient Blueberry Protein Muffins

Servings:6

Cooking Time: 20 Minutes

Ingredients:
- 1 bananas
- 1 cup quinoa (cooked)
- 1/4 cup Greek vanilla yogurt (nonfat)
- 1/4 cup almond butter
- 1 cup blueberries (fresh)

Directions:
1. Preheat oven to 375°F. Spray 6 muffin cups with cooking spray. In large bowl, stir together banana, quinoa, nonfat yogurt and almond butter until blended. Fold in blueberries.
2. Spoon batter into prepared muffin cups. Bake for 20 to 25 minutes or until golden brown and set in center. Let cool completely.

Nutrition facts:

Calories Per Serving 140; Total Fat: 7g; Sodium: 30mg; Total Carbs: 14g; Fiber: 3g; Sugars: 7g; Protein: 5g

Blueberry Almond Pancakes

Servings:6

Cooking Time: 25 Minutes

Ingredients:
- 2 eggs
- 2 egg whites
- 3/4 cup light ricotta cheese
- 1/2 tsp vanilla extract
- 1/4 cup unsweetened vanilla almond milk
- 1 large ripe banana
- 1 lemon (juiced and zested)
- 1 cup almond flour
- 1/2 cup ground flax seed
- 1 tsp baking powder
- 1 nonstick cooking spray
- 1/2 cup blueberries

Directions:
1. Add the eggs, egg whites, ricotta cheese, vanilla, almond milk, banana, lemon juice, and lemon zest to a blender. Blend until smooth.
2. In a small bowl, combine the almond flour, ground flax seed, and baking powder. Add the dry mixture to the liquid mixture in the blender and blend until smooth.
3. Coat a nonstick saute pan with cooking spray and place over medium heat. Scoop a scant 1/3 cup of the pancake batter into the pan and top with 4-5 blueberries. Let cook until the edges begin to brown (2-3 minutes); then flip the pancake to continue to cook an additional 2-3 minutes. Remove from the pan and repeat the process for the remaining 5 pancakes.

Nutrition facts:

Calories Per Serving 240; Total Fat: 16g; Sodium: 200mg; Total Carbs: 16g; Fiber: 6g; Sugars: 6g; Protein: 13g

Keto Chocolate Cake Recipe

Servings: 20

Cooking Time: 45 Minutes

Ingredients:
- 1 ¾ cups almond flour
- 2 cups erythritol
- ¾ cup natural unsweetened cocoa powder
- 2 ¼ tsp baking soda
- ½ tsp baking powder
- 1 tsp salt
- 1 cup milk, low fat
- ½ cup vegetable oil
- 1 ½ tsp vanilla extract
- 4 large eggs
- ½ cup hot water
- Frosting Ingredients
- 1 cup heavy cream
- 1 tsp vanilla
- 1 tbsp erythritol or preferred sweetener

Directions:
1. In a large bowl, mix together dry ingredients.
2. In a medium bowl, whisk eggs, then add milk, vanilla, and oil.
3. Add liquid ingredients into dry ingredients to create batter. Add in ½ cup warm water. Mix evenly.
4. Pour batter into greased 9x13 cake pan. Bake at 350 F for 45 minutes or until the toothpick comes out clean.
5. Instructions for Frosting
6. In a large bowl, whip cream until stiff peaks are just about to form.
7. Beat in vanilla and sweetener until peaks form.

Nutrition facts:
Calories Per Serving: 170; Total Fat: 16g; Sodium: 268mg; Total Carbs: 6g; Fiber: 2g; Sugars: 1g; Protein: 5g

Almond, Wild Blueberry, And Flax Smoothie

Servings: 3

Ingredients:
- 1 1/2 cup fresh or frozen wild blueberries
- 1 1/2 cup DIY Nut Milk or organic, unsweetened almond milk
- 2 tbsp almond flour
- 3 tbsp ground flax seed
- 1 tbsp packed fresh mint leaves
- 2 lime juice (freshly squeezed)
- 2 raw honey
- 1 cup ice

Directions:
1. In a blender, combine all ingredients and purée until smooth.
2. Divide smoothie among 3 glasses and enjoy immediately.

Nutrition facts:
Calories Per Serving 160; Total Fat: 8g; Sodium: 15mg; Total Carbs: 21g; Fiber: 6g; Sugars: 12g; Protein: 5g

Instant Pot Chia Berry Crepes

Servings: 4

Cooking Time: 5 Minutes

Ingredients:
- 1 cup frozen blueberries
- 1 cup frozen raspberries
- 1/2 cup plus 1 tbsp water (divided use)
- 2 tsp chia seeds
- 2 tsp Cornstarch
- 3 tbsp powdered sugar (divided use)
- 1/8 tsp almond extract
- 4 premade crepes

- 1 cup plain 2% Greek yogurt

Directions:
1. Place the berries, 1/2 cup of the water, and the chia seeds in the Instant Pot. Seal the lid, close the valve, and set the Manual/Pressure Cook button to 1 minute.
2. Use a quick pressure release. When the valve drops, carefully remove the lid.
3. In a small bowl, stir together the remaining 1 Tbsp of water and the cornstarch. Stir until the cornstarch is dissolved.
4. Press the Cancel button and set to Sauté. Then press the Adjust button to "More" or "High." Stir the cornstarch mixture into the berries. Bring to a boil and boil for 1 minute, or until thickened slightly.
5. Turn off the heat. Stir in 2 Tbsp of the powdered sugar and the almond extract. Place the berry mixture in a medium bowl and let stand for 15 minutes to cool slightly.
6. Spoon equal amounts of the berry mixture down the center of each crepe (about 1/3 cup per crepe). Fold the ends over to overlap slightly. Spoon the remaining 1 Tbsp of powdered sugar into a fine mesh sieve and sprinkle evenly over each crepe. Top each crepe with 1/4 cup yogurt and serve immediately.

Nutrition facts:
Calories Per Serving 170; Total Fat: 3g; Sodium: 105mg; Total Carbs: 28g; Fiber: 4g; Sugars: 17g; Protein: 8g

No-bake Peanut Butter & Chocolate Bites

Servings:24

Ingredients:
- 1/3 cup low calorie granulated sugar blend, such as Splenda sugar blend
- 1/3 cup skim milk
- 1/2 cup peanut butter
- 1 tsp vanilla extract
- 2 cup old-fashioned rolled oats (not quick cooking)
- 3 tbsp mini-chocolate chips

Directions:
1. In a small saucepan, combine sugar blend and milk over medium heat. Stir well and bring to a boil for 1 1/2 minutes. Stir in peanut butter and vanilla.
2. Remove from heat and add oats. Stir until oats are evenly coated in the peanut mixture and everything has cooled. Fold in the chocolate chips.
3. Scoop oat mixture into 1 Tbsp. balls and place on waxed paper. Let cool and refrigerate.

Nutrition facts:
Calories Per Serving 80; Total Fat: 3.5g; Sodium: 20mg; Total Carbs: 9g; Fiber:1g; Sugars: 4g; Protein:2g

Chocolate Walnut Mug Cake

Servings:1
Cooking Time: 1 Minutes

Ingredients:
- 2 tbsp unsweetened cocoa powder
- 2 tbsp white whole-wheat flour
- 1 Nonstick cooking spray
- 1/4 tsp baking powder
- 1 pinch pinch salt
- 1 1/2 tsp stevia powder

- 1 1/2 tsp canola oil
- 2 tbsp skim milk
- 1/4 tsp vanilla extract
- 3/4 tbsp walnuts (chopped)

Directions:
1. Spray a coffee mug with cooking spray.
2. Add the flour, cocoa powder, baking powder, salt, stevia, canola oil, milk and vanilla and stir to combine.
3. Microwave for 45 seconds.
4. Top with the walnuts and serve.

Nutrition facts:
Calories Per Serving 200; Total Fat: 12g; Sodium: 250mg; Total Carbs: 22g; Fiber: 5g; Sugars: 2g; Protein: 6g

Air Fryer Keto Blueberry Muffins

Servings:6
Cooking Time: 5 Minutes

Ingredients:
- 1 cup almond flour
- 2 tablespoons powdered erythritol
- 1/4 cup milk
- 1 large egg
- 1 teaspoon baking powder
- 1/2 teaspoon salt
- 1 cup blueberries

Directions:
1. In a large bowl mix together the almond flour, erythritol, milk, egg baking powder, and salt.
2. Mix well.
3. Stir in the blueberries.
4. Pour the mixture into a greased silicone cup of a muffin tin.
5. Place the silicone cups or muffin tin into the air fryer basket or onto the air fryer tray.
6. Set the temperature to 320 degrees F, for 5 minutes.
7. Plate, serve and enjoy!

Nutrition facts:
Calories Per Serving: 138; Total Fat: 10g; Sodium: 280mg; Total Carbs: 8g; Fiber: 3g; Sugars: 4g; Protein:6g

Fruit And Almond Smoothie

Servings:2

Ingredients:
- 1 cup frozen strawberries and peaches
- 1/2 cup Plain Nonfat Greek yogurt
- 1 cup unsweetened almond milk

Directions:
1. Combine all ingredients in a blender and puree until smooth and thick.

Nutrition facts:
Calories Per Serving 100; Total Fat: 2.5g; Sodium: 110mg; Total Carbs: 15g; Fiber: 2g; Protein: 5g

Easiest Low Carb Blondie Mug Cake With Prune Glaze

Servings:1
Cooking Time: 2 Minutes

Ingredients:
- 2 Tbs almond flour
- 1 Tbs vanilla protein powder
- ¼ tsp baking powder
- 2 Tbs Sunsweet Amaz!n Prune Juice
- 1 egg
- Glaze
- ¼ cup sugar-free confectioner 'sugar' with erythritol

- 3 tsp Sunsweet Amaz!n Prune Juice

Directions:

1. Mug cake instructions:
2. In a small bowl, mix together dry ingredients. Whisk egg in separate bowl. Add egg and juice to dry ingredients to create batter.
3. Place batter into a greased mug or ramakin. Microwave on high 1.5 to 2 minutes until mug cake holds its shape and a toothpick comes out clean. If cake is slightly mushy, microwave in 30 second intervals until desired consistency is achieved.
4. Glaze instructions:
5. In a small bowl, add sweetener and add prune juice teaspoon by teaspoon while stirring until glaze reaches desired consistency. Drizzle over mug cake and enjoy!

Nutrition facts:

Calories Per Serving: 209; Total Fat: 12g; Sodium: 395mg; Total Carbs: 13g; Fiber: 2.5g; Sugars: 6g; Protein: 13.5g

Peppermint Chocolate "nice Cream"

Servings:3

Ingredients:

- 2 med fully ripened bananas (sliced into coins and frozen)
- 3 tbsp unsweetened cocoa powder
- 1/2 tsp vanilla extract
- 1/4 tsp peppermint extract
- 1 tbsp cacao nibs

Directions:

1. Add the frozen banana coins, cocoa powder, and extracts to a food processor. Cover and pulse 10 times to chop the bananas.
2. Process the banana mixture on high speed until creamy, about 2½ minutes. Every 30 seconds, stop and scrape down the inside of the food processor.
3. Add the cacao nibs and pulse 3 times to combine.
4. Enjoy immediately, soft-serve style. Or freeze until solid; at serving time, set it out for 15 minutes, scoop, and serve.

Nutrition facts:

Calories Per Serving 110; Total Fat: 2.5g; Sodium: 0mg; Total Carbs: 24g; Fiber: 5g; Sugars: 11g; Protein: 2g

Instant Pot Almond-toffee Topped Pears

Servings:4

Cooking Time: 11 Minutes

Ingredients:

- 1/4 cup slivered almonds
- 8 sugar-free caramel-flavored hard candies (such as Werther's) (crushed)
- 1 pinch salt
- 3/4 cup water
- 1/4 cup apple juice
- 1 cinnamon stick
- 2 firm pears (peeled, halved lengthwise, and cored)
- 1 tsp light butter with canola oil
- 1/2 tsp vanilla extract

Directions:

1. Press the Sauté button on the multicooker. When the pot is hot, add the almonds and cook for 4 minutes, stirring occasionally. Set aside to cool, then coarsely chop.
2. In a small bowl, add the chopped almonds, crushed candies, and salt. Set aside.

3. Place the water, juice, and cinnamon stick in the multicooker pot. Place the steamer basket in the pot and arrange the pears on top of it.
4. Seal the lid, close the valve, and press the Cancel button. Select Manual and cook for 2 minutes. (If you prefer a very tender pear, cook an additional minute.) Use a quick pressure release.
5. When the valve drops, carefully remove the lid. Remove the steamer basket and pears. Place the pears, cut side up, in four dessert bowls. Remove and discard the cinnamon stick.
6. Press the Cancel button, then press the Sauté button. Bring the liquid in the pot to a boil. Boil for 3 minutes, or until the liquid is reduced to ¼ cup. Stir in the butter, vanilla extract, and almond-candy mixture. Cook for 30 seconds, or until the toffee has melted, stirring constantly.
7. Working quickly, spoon about 4 tsp of the toffee sauce into the center of each pear half.

Nutrition facts:

Calories Per Serving 130; Total Fat: 5g; Sodium: 80mg; Total Carbs: 22g; Fiber: 4g; Sugars: 11g; Protein:2g

Strawberry-lemon Cheesecake

Servings:4

Ingredients:
- 1 graham cracker (crumbled)
- 2 cup strawberries (sliced)
- 1/2 tsp ground cinnamon
- 1 lemon
- 3/4 tsp honey
- 1 1/2 cup ricotta cheese (nonfat)

Directions:
1. In a small bowl, mix together the ricotta cheese, honey, lemon zest, and cinnamon.
2. Divide the mixture among four individual dessert dishes. Top each dish with a portion of strawberries and sprinkle with some of the graham cracker crumbs.

Nutrition facts:

Calories Per Serving 115; Total Fat: 0.5g; Sodium: 90mg; Total Carbs: 17g; Fiber: 2g; Sugars: 11g; Protein: 11g

Carrot Cake Whoopie Pies

Servings:12

Cooking Time: 15 Minutes

Ingredients:
- 1 nonstick cooking spray
- 1/2 cup low-calorie brown sugar blend (such as Truvia or Splenda)
- 1/2 cup unsweetened applesauce
- 1/4 cup olive oil
- 1/2 cup egg substitute
- 1 tsp vanilla extract
- 1 cup whole wheat flour
- 1 cup old-fashioned rolled oats (not quick cooking)
- 2 tsp baking powder
- 1/2 tsp baking soda
- 1 tsp ground cinnamon
- 1/4 tsp ground nutmeg
- 2 cup shredded carrots
- 8 oz fat-free cream cheese
- 1 tsp vanilla extract
- 2 tbsp maple syrup
- 2 tbsp low-calorie granulated sugar substitute (such as Truvia)
- 1 tsp lemon juice

Directions:
1. Preheat the oven to 350 degrees F. Line two baking sheets with parchment paper and coat with cooking spray. Set aside.

2. In a medium bowl, combine the brown sugar blend, applesauce, oil, egg substitute, and vanilla. Mix well and set aside.
3. In a large bowl, combine the flour, oats, baking powder, baking soda, cinnamon, and nutmeg.
4. Make a well in the center of the dry ingredients. Add the sugar (wet) mixture to he dry ingredients all at once and mix well.
5. Stir in the carrots. Scoop mounds of batter the size of a heaping tablespoon onto the baking sheets. Space them about 2 inches apart for a total of 24 cookies (2 sheets of 12).
6. Bake 15 minutes. Set aside to cool.
7. In a small bowl, beat the filling ingredients until smooth and fluffy. Spread a light layer of frosting between two cookies.

Nutrition facts:

Calories Per Serving 160; Total Fat: 5g; Sodium: 270mg; Total Carbs: 23g; Fiber: 3g; Sugars: 9g; Protein: 6g

Banana Chocolate "ice Cream"

Servings:8

Cooking Time: 35 Minutes

Ingredients:

- 2 medium bananas
- 1/3 cup skim milk
- 2 tbsp cocoa powder
- 1 cup whipped topping (fat-free)

Directions:

1. Peel bananas and slice into 1/4-inch coins. Place in a bowl and freeze for at least 2 hours.
2. Once bananas are frozen, add the bananas, milk and cocoa powder to blender. Blend until smooth.
3. Fold in the whipped topping.
4. Place mixture in a freezer-safe container and freeze for at least 30 minutes.
5. Scoop into 1/2-cup scoops to serve.

Nutrition facts:

Calories Per Serving 80; Total Fat: 0.5g; Sodium: 15mg; Total Carbs: 18g; Fiber:2g; Sugars: 9g; Protein: 2g

VEGETABLES RECIPES

Keto Air Fryer Zucchini Fries

Servings: 4
Cooking Time: 10 Minutes

Ingredients:
- 2 medium zucchini
- 1 large egg beaten
- ⅓ cup almond flour
- ½ cup parmesan cheese grated
- 1 tsp Italian seasoning
- ½ tsp garlic powder
- ¼ tsp sea salt
- ¼ tsp black pepper
- olive oil cooking spray

Directions:
1. Cut the zucchini in half and then into sticks about ½ inch thick and 3-4 inches long.
2. In a bowl, combine the almond flour, grated parmesan, Italian seasoning, garlic powder, sea salt, and black pepper. Mix to combine. Set aside.
3. In a separate bowl, whisk egg until beaten.
4. Dredge zucchini sticks in the egg wash and then roll and coat in the almond flour breading mixture. Place on a plate (for air fryer) or a lined baking sheet (for the oven).
5. Generously spray the zucchini sticks with olive oil cooking spray.

Nutrition facts:
Calories Per Serving 117; Total Fat: 8g; Sodium: 399mg; Total Carbs: 6g; Fiber: 1g; Sugars: 3g; Protein: 7g

Instant Pot Vegetarian Thai Mushroom Soup

Servings: 4

Ingredients:
- 8 oz sliced mushrooms, preferably cremini (baby bella)
- 2 cup frozen pepper-and-onion blend
- 1 (15-oz) can no-salt-added chickpeas (rinsed and drained)
- 1 (14.5-oz) can no-salt-added diced tomatoes
- 1/2 cup water
- 1 tbsp sriracha
- 1/2 tsp ground cumin
- 1 1/2 cup lite coconut milk
- 1/2 cup chopped fresh cilantro
- 1 tbsp sugar
- 1 tbsp grated fresh ginger
- 1/2 tsp salt

Directions:
1. Combine the mushrooms, frozen vegetables, chickpeas, tomatoes, water, sriracha, and cumin in the multicooker pot.
2. Seal the lid and close the valve. Select Manual and cook for 8 minutes. Use a quick pressure release.
3. When the valve drops, carefully remove the lid and stir in the remaining ingredients. Let sit for 5 minutes to allow the flavors to blend. Serve warm.

Nutrition facts:
Calories Per Serving 240; Total Fat: 7g; Sodium: 440mg; Total Carbs: 35g; Fiber: 7g; Sugars: 13g; Protein: 12g

Lentil Chili

Servings: 6

Ingredients:
- 2 tablespoons extra-virgin olive oil
- 3 medium poblano peppers, seeded and chopped
- 1 medium white onion, chopped, plus more for garnish
- ¼ cup tomato paste
- 5 cloves garlic, finely chopped
- 1 tablespoon chili powder
- 1 tablespoon ground cumin
- 2 teaspoons smoked paprika
- 5 cups water
- 2 (14.5 ounce) cans no-salt-added diced tomatoes
- 1 ½ cups dried red lentils
- ½ cup finely chopped fresh cilantro leaves and tender stems, plus more for garnish
- ¾ teaspoon salt

Directions:
1. Heat oil in a large Dutch oven over medium-high heat. Add poblanos and onion; cook, stirring occasionally, until the onion is softened and translucent, 7 to 8 minutes. Add tomato paste, garlic, chili powder, cumin and smoked paprika; cook, stirring often, until the mixture is very fragrant and the garlic softens slightly, about 2 minutes.
2. Add water and tomatoes; bring to a boil over high heat. Stir in lentils; return to a boil. Reduce heat to medium; simmer, stirring occasionally, until the lentils are tender, 20 to 25 minutes. Stir in cilantro and salt. Divide the chili among 6 bowls. Top each with chopped onion and cilantro, if desired.
3. To make ahead
4. Refrigerate in an airtight container for up to 5 days or freeze for up to 2 months.

Nutrition facts:
Calories Per Serving 280; Total Fat: 6g; Sodium: 430mg; Total Carbs: 46g; Fiber: 9g; Sugars: 7g; Protein: 14g

Air-fryer Zucchini

Servings: 4

Ingredients:
- 2 tablespoons grated Parmesan cheese
- 1 tablespoon extra-virgin olive oil
- ½ teaspoon dried oregano
- ½ teaspoon salt
- ¼ teaspoon garlic powder
- ¼ teaspoon onion powder
- ¼ teaspoon ground pepper
- ⅛ teaspoon crushed red pepper
- 2 large (8-ounce) zucchini, sliced 1/4-inch thick
- 2 teaspoons lemon juice

Directions:
1. Preheat air fryer to 400°F for 5 minutes. Combine Parmesan, oil, oregano, salt, garlic powder, onion powder, pepper and crushed red pepper in a medium bowl. Add zucchini and toss to coat.
2. Working in batches if necessary, arrange the zucchini slices in a single layer in the fryer basket. Cook, flipping once, until golden brown, 10 to 12 minutes. Sprinkle with lemon juice and serve with lemon wedges.

Nutrition facts:
Calories Per Serving 64; Total Fat: 5g; Sodium: 345mg; Total Carbs: 5g; Fiber: 1g; protein 2g

Bacon-wrapped Asparagus In The Air Fryer

Servings: 6-8
Cooking Time: 12 Minutes

Ingredients:
- 1 bunch of asparagus
- 1 pound of bacon (regular sliced not thick)

Directions:
1. Wash and trim the ends of your asparagus.
2. Preheat your air fryer to 400 degrees F.
3. Wrap one slice of bacon around one stalk of asparagus.
4. Lay your bacon-wrapped asparagus in your air fryer. If possible lay the ends of your bacon down flat to help keep them from curling. Leave space between your stalks so the air can circulate around them. I tried to do my first batch with my thicker stalks and they cooked for 12 minutes. Then in my second batch, I cooked my thinner ones for 10 minutes.
5. Serve and enjoy.

Nutrition facts:
Calories Per Serving 266; Total Fat: 20g; Sodium: 955mg; Total Carbs: 1g; Fiber: 0g; Sugars: 0g; Protein: 19g

Slow-cooker Spinach Artichoke Dip

Servings: 16

Ingredients:
- 1 (16 ounce) bag frozen chopped spinach, thawed and squeezed dry
- 1 (14 ounce) can artichoke hearts, drained and chopped
- 8 ounces reduced-fat cream cheese, cut into cubes
- 8 ounces reduced-fat sour cream
- ½ cup shredded whole-milk mozzarella cheese
- ½ cup grated Parmesan cheese
- ½ teaspoon garlic powder
- ¼ teaspoon crushed red pepper
- ¼ teaspoon salt
- ¼ teaspoon ground pepper
- 4 cups sliced vegetables, such as carrots and bell peppers
- 16 slices whole-wheat baguette (1/2 inch thick), toasted

Directions:
1. Combine spinach, artichoke hearts, cream cheese, sour cream, mozzarella, Parmesan, garlic powder, crushed red pepper, salt and pepper in a 4-quart slow cooker. Cook on High for 2 hours. Stir and serve with sliced vegetables and baguette slices.

Nutrition facts:
Calories Per Serving 169; Total Fat: 7g; Sodium: 379mg; Total Carbs: 21g; Fiber: 2g; Sugars: 2g; Protein: 7g

Vegetarian Sliders With Black Beans, Chard & Poblanos

Servings: 8

Ingredients:
- 1 cup boiling water
- 1 tablespoon honey
- ¾ teaspoon salt, divided
- 1 cup cider vinegar
- 1 small red onion, thinly sliced
- 3 medium poblano peppers
- 1 tablespoon extra-virgin olive oil, divided
- 1 medium yellow onion, diced

- 3 cloves garlic, minced
- 1 bunch chard, including stems, chopped (8 cups)
- 4 ½ cups cooked or canned (rinsed) black beans, patted dry
- 1 large egg, lightly beaten
- ½ cup fine dry whole-wheat breadcrumbs
- 2 teaspoons Creole seasoning, plus more for serving
- Cooking spray
- 16 slider buns, preferably whole-wheat, split and toasted
- 1 cup crumbled feta cheese

Directions:

1. Combine boiling water, honey and 1/2 teaspoon salt in a heatproof bowl, stirring to dissolve the honey and salt. Stir in vinegar, then add red onion. Set aside.
2. Position rack in upper third of oven; preheat broiler to high. Place peppers on a baking sheet and broil, turning occasionally, until blackened on all sides, 12 to 15 minutes. Transfer to a bowl, cover with plastic wrap and let steam until cool enough to handle, about 15 minutes. Peel and seed the peppers. Slice or tear them into strips; set aside.
3. Meanwhile, heat 1 1/2 teaspoons oil in a large skillet over medium heat. Add yellow onion and cook, stirring occasionally, until soft and light golden brown, 3 to 5 minutes. Add garlic; cook, stirring occasionally, until fragrant and soft, 1 to 2 minutes. Scrape onto a plate.
4. Return the pan to medium heat and add the remaining 1 1/2 teaspoons oil and chard. Cook, stirring frequently and adding a splash of water if it starts to stick, until the stems are tender and any liquid has evaporated, 5 to 8 minutes. Scrape onto the plate and let cool, about 10 minutes.
5. Place beans in a large bowl and coarsely mash. Add the chard mixture, egg, breadcrumbs, Creole seasoning and the remaining 1/4 teaspoon salt; mix well.
6. Coat a baking sheet with cooking spray. Using about 1/3 cup to make each, portion the bean mixture into 16 patties, 1/2 inch thick, and place on the prepared baking sheet. Coat the patties lightly with cooking spray. Broil until browned and firm on top, 6 to 8 minutes. Flip the patties and coat the other side with cooking spray. Broil until browned, 4 to 6 minutes more.
7. Serve the patties in buns, topped with the reserved peppers, pickled onion and feta. Sprinkle with more Creole seasoning, if desired.

Nutrition facts:

Calories Per Serving457; Total Fat: 13g; Sodium: 564mg; Total Carbs: 72g; Fiber: 11g; Sugars: 9g; Protein: 23g

Ham And Broccoli Frittata

Servings:4
Cooking Time: 25 Minutes

Ingredients:

- 1 nonstick cooking spray
- 2 cup packaged hash brown potatoes or fresh grated potato
- 9 oz small broccoli florets (rinsed and drained, but not dried—some water droplets should cling to the broccoli)
- 4 eggs
- 4 egg whites
- 2 oz lower-sodium, low-fat ham (cut into 1/4-inch cubes)
- 1/4 cup skim milk
- 1/4 tsp black pepper

Directions:

1. Preheat the oven to 400°F.

2. Lightly spray a medium ovenproof skillet with cooking spray. Heat over medium heat. Remove from the heat. Put the potatoes in the skillet. Lightly spray with cooking spray. Cook for 4–5 minutes, or until the potatoes are golden brown, stirring occasionally.
3. Put the broccoli in a microwaveable bowl. Microwave, covered, on 100% power (high) for 4 to 5 minutes, or until tender-crisp. Drain in a colander. Stir the broccoli into the potatoes.
4. In a medium bowl, whisk together the egg whites and eggs. Whisk in the ham, milk, and pepper. Pour the mixture over the potatoes and broccoli, stirring well.
5. Bake for 15–18 minutes, or until the eggs are set (it shouldn't jiggle when the frittata is gently shaken). Let cool for at least 10 minutes, then cut into 4 equal slices.

Nutrition facts:

Calories Per Serving 170; Total Fat: 6g; Sodium: 290mg; Total Carbs: 14g; Fiber: 3g; Sugars: 3g; Protein: 15g

Vegetarian Antipasto Sliders

Servings: 6

Ingredients:

- 1 12-count package pull-apart dinner rolls, preferably whole-wheat
- 2 tablespoons mayonnaise
- 2 tablespoons prepared pesto
- 1 cup canned quartered artichoke hearts, rinsed and patted dry
- ½ cup sliced roasted red bell peppers, rinsed and patted dry
- ¼ cup chopped pepperoncini, rinsed and patted dry
- 4 slices provolone cheese
- 2 teaspoons extra-virgin olive oil
- ¼ teaspoon Italian seasoning

Directions:

1. Preheat oven to 350°F.
2. Being careful to not separate the rolls, use a serrated knife to cut horizontally through them all. Place the bottom halves in a 9-by-13-inch baking dish. Combine mayonnaise and pesto in a small bowl; spread over the bottom halves. Top with artichoke hearts, peppers, pepperoncini and cheese. Cover with the top halves of the rolls. Brush the tops with oil and sprinkle with Italian seasoning.
3. Bake until the cheese is melted, 10 to 15 minutes. Let cool for 5 minutes, then pull apart to serve.

Nutrition facts:

Calories Per Serving 320; Total Fat: 16 g; Sodium: 805mg; Total Carbs: 32g; Fiber: 3g; Sugars: 1g; Protein: 11g

Air-fryer Fried Green Tomatoes

Servings: 8

Ingredients:

- 3 medium green tomatoes, sliced 1/4-inch thick
- ¼ teaspoon salt plus 1/8 teaspoon, divided
- ¼ cup all-purpose flour
- 1 teaspoon garlic powder
- 2 large eggs, lightly beaten
- ½ cup whole-wheat panko breadcrumbs
- ½ cup cornmeal
- Avocado oil cooking spray
- ¼ teaspoon ground pepper
- ½ cup mayonnaise
- 2 tablespoons chopped fresh parsley

- 1 tablespoon whole-grain mustard
- 1 tablespoon lemon juice
- 2 teaspoons capers, rinsed
- 1 teaspoon Worcestershire sauce

Directions:

1. Pat tomato slices dry with paper towels. Sprinkle with 1/4 teaspoon salt.
2. Stir flour and garlic powder together in a shallow dish. Place eggs in a separate shallow dish. Stir panko and cornmeal together in a third shallow dish. Dredge the tomato slices in the flour mixture and then dip in the eggs, shaking off excess; dredge in the panko mixture.
3. Preheat air fryer to 400°F. Arrange half of the tomato slices in an even layer in the fryer basket; coat the tomatoes well with cooking spray. Cook until crispy and golden on one side, about 4 minutes. Flip the tomato slices; coat with cooking spray and cook until golden and crispy, about 4 minutes. Transfer to a plate. Repeat the procedure with the remaining tomatoes. Sprinkle evenly with pepper and the remaining 1/8 teaspoon salt.
4. Meanwhile, combine mayonnaise, parsley, mustard, lemon juice, capers and Worcestershire in a small bowl. Serve the tomatoes with the sauce.

Nutrition facts:

Calories Per Serving197; Total Fat:12 g; Sodium:369 mg; Total Carbs: 18g; Fiber: 2g; Sugars: 4g; Protein:5 g

Air Fried Cabbage

Servings:4

Cooking Time: 10 Minutes

Ingredients:

- 1 head cabbage
- 2 tbsp olive oil
- 1 tsp coarse sea salt
- 1 tsp fresh ground pepper
- 1 tbsp Old Bay Garlic & Herb seasoning

Directions:

1. slice cabbage into 2" slices – then quarter the slices 1 head cabbage places pie shaped slices into air fryer drizzle olive oil over all slices of cabbage 2 tbsp olive oil sprinkle salt, pepper and Old Bay on cabbage 1 tsp coarse sea salt,1 tsp fresh ground pepper,1 tbsp Old Bay Garlic & Herb seasoning air fry at 375 for 5 minutes toss cabbage with tongs – pieces will fall apart into large chunks air fry 3-4 additional minutes

Nutrition facts:

Calories Per Serving 105; Total Fat: 7.2g; Sodium: 272mg; Total Carbs: 10.4g; Fiber: 4.5g; Sugars: 5.7g; Protein: 2.3g

Keto Vegetarian Lasagna

Servings:5

Cooking Time: 50 Minutes

Ingredients:

- 3 medium sized zucchini
- 1 cup part-skim mozzarella cheese, shredded
- basil leaves, to garnish
- To make sauce
- 1 tbsp olive oil
- 1 tbsp garlic, chopped

- ½ yellow onion, diced
- 15 oz crushed tomatoes, canned
- 1 tsp Italian seasonings
- 1 tsp black pepper
- ½ tsp salt
- 5-6 basil leaves, roughly chopped
- To make filling
- 1½ cup part-skim ricotta cheese
- 1 egg
- ½ cup parmesan cheese, shredded
- ½ tsp black pepper
- ½ tsp salt

Directions:

1. Preheat the oven to 350 degrees F. Line a baking tray with parchment paper and keep it aside.
2. Trim the ends and slice the zucchini lengthwise to uniform strips using a mandolin. Not too thick and not too thin.
3. Place the zucchini strips on the prepared baking sheets next to each other and bake them for 20 minutes by flipping them to the other side halfway through. Once done, set aside to cool.
4. Meanwhile, prepare the sauce by heating a medium skillet with olive oil and garlic; saute for a minute and add onion. Cook the onion for 2-3 minutes and add the crushed tomato, Italian seasoning, basil, pepper and salt.
5. Simmer the sauce and cook for 5 minutes. Once done keep the sauce aside.
6. Prepare the filling by combining the ricotta, parmesan, egg, black pepper and salt in a bowl. Mix it and set aside.
7. For assembling the lasagna; add 2 tablespoons of prepared sauce on a 9X5 baking dish. Arrange a layer of pre baked zucchini strips. Add ⅓ cup of prepared ricotta filling followed by ¼ cup saucer and ¼ cup of mozzarella cheese. Repeat the same for three layers.
8. For the final layer end with zucchini strips and add the remaining cheese on top and cover the lasagna with aluminium foil. Bake the lasagna for 30 minutes at 350 degrees F.
9. Remove the foil and bake further for 10 more minutes until the cheese is melted.
10. Allow the zucchini lasagna to cool for 10 minutes. Before serving, slice the lasagna and serve while it is still warm.

Nutrition facts:

Calories Per Serving 292; Total Fat: 16g; Sodium: 991mg; Total Carbs: 17g; Fiber: 3g; Sugars: 8g; Protein: 22g

Sweet Potato Hash Stuffed Portobello Mushrooms

Servings:4

Ingredients:

- 4 large portobello mushrooms
- 3 tablespoons extra-virgin olive oil, divided
- ¾ teaspoon salt, divided
- ½ teaspoon ground pepper, divided
- 1 large sweet potato, peeled and diced
- ¼ cup water
- 1 large apple, peeled and diced
- 1 medium red bell pepper, diced
- ½ cup chopped shallots
- 1 teaspoon poultry seasoning
- ½ cup chopped walnuts, toasted
- 1 tablespoon chopped fresh parsley

Directions:

1. Preheat oven to 425°F.

2. Remove stems from mushrooms. Set the caps aside and chop the stems.
3. Lightly brush the mushroom caps with 1 tablespoon oil. Sprinkle with 1/4 teaspoon salt and 1/4 teaspoon pepper. Place on a rimmed baking sheet and roast until soft, 10 to 15 minutes. Keep warm.
4. Meanwhile, heat 1 tablespoon oil in a large skillet over medium heat. Add sweet potato and water. Cover and cook, stirring occasionally, until just cooked through, 6 to 8 minutes. Uncover and stir in the remaining 1 tablespoon oil, the chopped mushroom stems, apple, bell pepper, shallots, poultry seasoning and the remaining 1/2 teaspoon salt and 1/4 teaspoon pepper. Cook, stirring, until soft, about 5 minutes. Stir in walnuts and parsley. Fill each mushroom cap with about 1 cup filling.

Nutrition facts:

Calories Per Serving313; Total Fat:21 g; Sodium:463 mg; Total Carbs: 29g; Fiber: 6g; Sugars: 12g; Protein: 6g

Broccoli Onion Latkes

Servings:4
Cooking Time: 10 Minutes

Ingredients:
- 3 cup fresh or frozen chopped broccoli florets
- 1/2 cup diced onion
- 2 eggs
- 2 tbsp all-purpose flour
- 2 tbsp olive oil

Directions:
1. Boil the diced broccoli in a small amount of water for 5 minutes, then drain thoroughly.
2. Break eggs into a medium bowl and beat. Add the flour and mix well. Add the broccoli and onion and stir into the flour/egg mixture until well mixed.
3. Heat olive oil in a frying pan over medium-high heat. Drop the mixture by spoonfuls into the hot oil, making 4 equal portions. Flatten with a spatula, and cook until golden brown on both sides (about 3-4 minutes per side).
4. Remove the latkes from the pan and drain on a paper towel to soak up extra oil. Serve hot.

Nutrition facts:

Calories Per Serving 135; Total Fat: 0g; Sodium: 50mg; Total Carbs: 8g; Fiber: 1.7g; Sugars: 2g; Protein: 5g

Vegan Cauliflower Buffalo Wings

Servings:8

Ingredients:
- Cooking spray
- 1 ¼ cups unsweetened plain almond milk
- 1 cup all-purpose flour
- ½ teaspoon cayenne pepper
- 2 tablespoons garlic powder, plus 1/2 teaspoon, divided
- 2 tablespoons onion powder, plus 1/2 teaspoon, divided
- 1 ¼ teaspoons ground pepper, divided
- 8 cups cauliflower florets (from 1 medium head)
- 2 cups panko breadcrumbs
- ¼ cup vegan mayonnaise
- 2 tablespoons chopped fresh dill
- 1 tablespoon cider vinegar
- 3 ½ tablespoons Buffalo-style hot sauce
- ¼ cup celery leaves (Optional)

Directions:

1. Preheat oven to 400 degrees F. Line a baking sheet with parchment paper; coat with cooking spray. Whisk almond milk, flour, cayenne, 2 tablespoons garlic powder, 2 tablespoons onion powder and 1 teaspoon pepper in a large bowl to form a loose batter. Add cauliflower; toss well to coat.
2. Place panko in another large bowl. Using a slotted spoon, remove the cauliflower from the batter, letting excess drip off. Add the cauliflower to the panko; toss to coat. Arrange the breaded cauliflower on the prepared pan; coat the cauliflower liberally with cooking spray. Bake until golden brown, 35 to 40 minutes.
3. Meanwhile, whisk mayonnaise, dill, vinegar and the remaining 1/2 teaspoon garlic powder, 1/2 teaspoon onion powder and 1/4 teaspoon pepper in a small bowl.
4. Arrange the cauliflower on a platter; drizzle with hot sauce. Drizzle the dressing over the cauliflower. Sprinkle with celery leaves, if desired.

Nutrition facts:

Calories Per Serving186; Total Fat: 6g; Sodium: 341mg; Total Carbs: 29g; Fiber: 3g; Sugars: 3g; Protein: 5g

Creamy Cauliflower-jalapeño Popper Dip

Servings:8

Ingredients:

- 1 (10 ounce) package frozen riced cauliflower, thawed and drained
- 1 cup nonfat plain Greek yogurt
- 1 (8 ounce) package reduced-fat cream cheese, softened
- 3 tablespoons grated Parmesan cheese
- ¼ cup whole-milk ricotta cheese
- ½ cup sliced pickled jalapeño peppers, drained
- ½ teaspoon kosher salt
- ½ teaspoon ground pepper
- Minced parsley for garnish
- Toasted baguette slices, crackers and/or sliced vegetables for dipping

Directions:

1. Preheat oven to 375°F.
2. Combine cauliflower, yogurt, cream cheese, Parmesan, ricotta, jalapeños, salt and pepper in a large bowl; mix well. Transfer to a 2-quart oven-safe baking dish. Bake until browned around the edges, 30 to 35 minutes.
3. Garnish with parsley, if desired. Serve immediately with toasted baguette slices, crackers and/or sliced vegetables for dipping.

Nutrition facts:

Calories Per Serving110; Total Fat: 6g; Sodium: 372mg; Total Carbs: 6g; Fiber: 1g; Sugars: 3g; Protein: 8g

Cheesy Black Bean & Corn-stuffed Portobello Mushrooms

Servings:4

Ingredients:

- 3 tablespoons extra-virgin olive oil, divided
- 1 teaspoon garlic powder, divided
- ⅛ teaspoon salt, plus 1/4 teaspoon, divided
- ¼ teaspoon ground pepper
- 4 portobello mushrooms (about 14 ounces), stems and gills removed
- ¼ cup finely chopped red onion
- 1 teaspoon ground cumin

- 1 cup frozen corn, thawe
- 1 cup reduced-sodium black beans, rinsed
- ¼ cup chopped fresh cilantro
- ½ cup shredded pepper Jack cheese

Directions:

1. Preheat oven to 400 degrees F.
2. Combine 2 tablespoons oil, 1/2 teaspoon garlic powder, 1/8 teaspoon salt and pepper in a small bowl. Using a silicone brush, coat mushrooms all over with the oil mixture. Place the mushrooms on a large rimmed baking sheet and bake until mostly soft, about 10 minutes.
3. Meanwhile, heat the remaining 1 tablespoon oil in a medium saucepan over medium-high heat. Add onion; cook, stirring, until almost soft, about 3 minutes. Add cumin and the remaining 1/2 teaspoon garlic powder and 1/4 teaspoon salt; stir until incorporated. Add corn and beans; cook, stirring, until hot. Remove from heat and stir in cilantro and cheese. Divide the mixture between the mushrooms and bake until the cheese is melted and the filling is heated through, 5 to 7 minutes. Serve with pico de gallo, if desired.

Nutrition facts:

Calories Per Serving258; Total Fat:15 g; Sodium: 365mg; Total Carbs: 24g; Fiber: 6g; Sugars: 6g; Protein: 9g

Low Carb Veggie Fried Rice Bowl

Servings:2
Cooking Time: 5 Minutes

Ingredients:

- 1 tbsp canola or other vegetable oil
- 1 cup diced cooked lean protein of your choice (such as chicken, pork, shrimp, tofu, etc)
- 3 tbsp chopped scallions or other onion
- 3/4 tsp grated fresh ginger (or 1/8 tsp ground ginger)
- 1/2 tsp (about 1 clove) minced garlic
- 1 1/2 cup assorted vegetables, chopped into bite-sized pieces (cooked or raw)
- 1 1/2 cup cauliflower "rice"
- 1 egg (beaten)
- 1 tbsp teriyaki sauce
- 2 tbsp chopped fresh cilantro

Directions:

1. Heat a nonstick wok or large skillet over medium-high heat. Add the oil and after about 20 seconds, add diced protein, onions, ginger, garlic, assorted veggies and riced cauliflower, stirring often with spoon or spatula, for about 2 minutes.
2. Reduce heat to medium and pull the mixture away from the center of the pan with a spatula and pour the beaten egg in the center. When it starts to cook, use a spatula to stir all of the fried rice ingredients together for about a minute to finish cooking the egg.
3. Sprinkle teriyaki sauce and cilantro over the top and gently stir just to blend flavors (about 1 minute more). Taste and add more teriyaki sauce if desired. Divide into two bowls and serve!

Nutrition facts:

Calories Per Serving 250; Total Fat: 12g; Sodium: 410mg; Total Carbs: 11g; Fiber: 4g; Sugars: 6g; Protein: 25g

Bolognese Zucchini Boats In The Air Fryer

Servings:4
Cooking Time: 22 Minutes

Ingredients:
- 2 Medium Zucchinis
- 300 g Pork Mince
- ½ Large Onion Diced
- 400 g Tinned Tomatoes
- 1 Tbsp Garlic Puree
- 2 Tsp Oregano
- 50 g Hard Cheese optional
- Salt & Pepper

Directions:
1. Place your minced pork, garlic, diced onion and a little salt and pepper into an air fryer cake pan. Cook for 8 minutes at 180c/360f in the air fryer.
2. Stir in tinned tomatoes and oregano and cook for a further 2 minutes at 200c/400f.
3. Slice the zucchini in half lengthways and remove centre from the zucchini using a spoon.
4. When the air fryer beeps load the cooked Bolognese into the zucchini boats and place the zucchini boats in the air fryer on the grill pan. Cook for a further 10 minutes at 180c/360f.
5. Once it beeps add cheese on top and cook for a further 2 minutes at 200c/400f.

Nutrition facts:
Calories Per Serving 309; Total Fat: 21g; Sodium: 261mg; Total Carbs: 13g; Fiber: 3g; Sugars: 8g; Protein: 19g

Air-fryer Red Potatoes

Servings:8

Ingredients:
- 2 pounds small unpeeled red potatoes, cut into wedges
- 2 tablespoons olive oil
- 1 tablespoon minced fresh rosemary or 1 teaspoon dried rosemary, crushed
- 2 garlic cloves, minced
- 1/2 teaspoon salt
- 1/4 teaspoon pepper

Directions:
1. Preheat air fryer to 400°. Drizzle potatoes with oil. Sprinkle with rosemary, garlic, salt and pepper; toss gently to coat.
2. Place on ungreased tray in air-fryer basket. Cook until potatoes are golden brown and tender, 10-12 minutes, stirring once.

Nutrition facts:
Calories Per Serving 111; Total Fat: 3.7g; Sodium: 154mg; Total Carbs: 18.4g; Fiber: 2.9g; Sugars: 1.3g; Protein: 2g

Air-fryer Zucchini Fritters

Servings:4

Ingredients:
- Cooking spray
- 2 medium zucchini
- 1 large egg, lightly beaten
- ½ cup grated Parmesan cheese
- ⅓ cup whole-wheat flour
- 1 teaspoon garlic powder
- 1 teaspoon onion powder
- ¼ teaspoon ground pepper

- ½ cup sour cream
- 2 tablespoons chopped fresh mint

Directions:

1. Preheat air fryer to 375°F for 10 minutes. Generously coat the fryer basket with cooking spray.
2. Grate zucchini on the large holes of a box grater over a clean kitchen towel. Gather the grated zucchini in the towel and squeeze over the sink to remove as much liquid as possible. Transfer the zucchini to a medium bowl. Add egg, Parmesan, flour, garlic powder, onion powder and pepper; stir until combined. Shape the mixture into 8 patties (about 3 inches wide).
3. Working in batches if necessary, coat the tops of the patties with cooking spray. Arrange them in a single layer in the fryer basket. Cook for 7 minutes; flip the patties and continue to cook until crisp and well browned, about 7 minutes more. Serve with sour cream and mint.

Nutrition facts:

Calories Per Serving 177; Total Fat: 10g; Sodium: 219mg; Total Carbs: 15g; Fiber: 3g; Sugars: 4g; Protein: 8g

Air-fryer Asparagus

Servings: 4

Ingredients:

- 1/4 cup mayonnaise
- 4 teaspoons olive oil
- 1-1/2 teaspoons grated lemon zest
- 1 garlic clove, minced
- 1/2 teaspoon pepper
- 1/4 teaspoon seasoned salt
- 1 pound fresh asparagus, trimmed
- 2 tablespoons shredded Parmesan cheese
- Lemon wedges, optional

Directions:

1. Preheat air fryer to 375°. In large bowl, combine the first 6 ingredients. Add asparagus; toss to coat. Working in batches, place in a single layer on greased tray in air-fryer basket.
2. Cook until tender and lightly browned, 4-6 minutes. Transfer to a serving platter; sprinkle with Parmesan cheese. If desired, serve with lemon wedges.

Nutrition facts:

Calories Per Serving 130 Total Fat: 10.3g; Sodium: 230mg; Total Carbs: 8.4g; Fiber: 2.5g; Sugars: 3.1g; Protein: 3.5g

Air Fryer Sweet Potato Nachos

Servings: 4

Cooking Time: 22 Minutes

Ingredients:

- 1 medium sweet potato (sliced into 1/8-inch thick chips)
- 1 nonstick cooking spray
- 1 1/2 cup frozen pepper-and-onion blend (partially thawed and drained)
- 1 jalapeño pepper (split lengthwise and seeded)
- 1/4 cup reduced-fat shredded cheddar or Mexican-style cheese
- 1/4 cup salsa
- 2/3 cup julienned or thinly sliced radishes
- 4 cherry tomatoes (cut into fourths)
- 1/2 cup shredded romaine lettuce
- 2 tbsp light sour cream
- 1 tbsp minced fresh cilantro

Directions:

1. Place the sweet potato slices evenly in the air fryer basket. Spray with nonstick cooking spray for 1

second. Spoon the frozen vegetables evenly over the potatoes. Place the jalapeño over the vegetables, skin side up. Spray with nonstick cooking spray for 1 second.

2. Set the temperature to 375° F and air fry for 20 minutes, or until the potatoes are cooked. They should be tender but crisp, not soft. Remove the jalapeño pepper and place it in a bowl; cover loosely with a kitchen towel and let stand for 5 minutes.
3. Sprinkle the cheese evenly over the vegetables. Air fry for 2 minutes, or until the cheese is melted.
4. Using the tip of a sharp knife, remove the browned or charred skin from the jalapeño pepper. Finely chop the pepper.
5. Using a spatula, lift the potatoes and vegetables out of the air fryer basket and arrange in an even layer on a serving platter. Sprinkle the chopped jalapeño over the vegetables. Top with the salsa, radishes, tomatoes, and lettuce. Add a dollop of sour cream and sprinkle of cilantro. Serve immediately.

Nutrition facts:

Calories Per Serving 100; Total Fat: 2.5g; Sodium: 180mg; Total Carbs:17g; Fiber: 3g; Sugars: 6g; Protein: 4g

Crispy Air Fryer Broccoli Bites With Nutritional Yeast

Servings:3-4
Cooking Time: 10 Minutes

Ingredients:
- 10 oz broccoli florets
- 1 Tablespoon avocado oil or olive oil
- 1 Tablespoon nutritional yeast
- Salt and pepper to taste
- 1 lemon (zest only)

Directions:
1. In a large bowl, whisk together the oil and nutritional yeast until well combined, season with salt and pepper to taste. Add the broccoli and toss until well covered
2. toss the ingredients in a bowl
3. Arrange in the air fryer. Set the air fryer to 350°F and cook for 8-10 minutes or until stems are tender, shaking the basket or stirring the broccoli halfway through.
4. arranged broccoli inside the air fryer basket
5. Grate zest from the lemon all over broccoli and serve.

Nutrition facts:

Calories Per Serving 98; Total Fat: 7g; Sodium: 31mg; Total Carbs: 8g; Fiber: 3g; Sugars: 2g; Protein: 3g

FISH AND SEAFOOD RECIPES

Air-fryer Bacon-wrapped Scallops

Servings:6

Ingredients:
- 12 medium sea scallops (about 9 ounces total)
- 3 thin center-cut bacon slices
- ¼ teaspoon ground pepper
- ¼ teaspoon paprika
- 1 teaspoon extra-virgin olive oil

Directions:
1. Preheat air fryer to 375°F. Pat scallops dry. Remove and discard the muscle from the side of each scallop. Cut bacon slices in half crosswise and then lengthwise to make 12 strips. Wrap 1 bacon strip around each scallop, overlapping the ends slightly. Thread a wooden pick through both ends of the bacon to secure it in place, pushing the pick through the opposite side of the scallop. Sprinkle the scallops evenly with pepper and paprika and brush lightly with oil.
2. Arrange the scallops in an even layer in the fryer basket. Cook until the bacon is beginning to crisp and the scallops are firm but tender, 10 to 12 minutes.

Nutrition facts:
Calories Per Serving43; Total Fat: 2g; Sodium: 178mg; Total Carbs: 1g; Protein: 5g

Tuna Ceviche

Servings:3

Ingredients:
- 5 oz low-sodium, water-packed tuna (drained)
- 1 tbsp chopped fresh cilantro
- 1/4 cup chopped red onion
- 1/4 tsp black pepper
- 1/4 tsp salt-free herb seasoning, such as Ms. Dash
- 3 tbsp lemon juice
- 18 low sodium saltine crackers

Directions:
1. Combine the tuna, onion, cilantro, black pepper, and seasoning blend in a small bowl. Add the lemon juice and mix everything together well. Cover and refrigerate for at least 2 hours to marinate before serving.

Nutrition facts:
Calories Per Serving 150; Total Fat: 4g; Sodium:160mg; Total Carbs: 16g; Fiber: 1g; Sugars: 1g; Protein: 13g

Air-fryer Crab Cakes

Servings:6

Ingredients:
- 2 large eggs
- 2 tablespoons unsalted butter, melted
- 1 tablespoon chopped fresh basil
- 2 teaspoons chopped fresh tarragon
- 2 teaspoons lower-sodium Worcestershire sauce

- 1 teaspoon grated lemon zest, plus lemon wedges for serving
- 1 teaspoon reduced-sodium Old Bay seasoning
- ½ teaspoon garlic powder
- ½ teaspoon onion powder
- ½ cup light sour cream, divided
- 2 tablespoons thinly sliced fresh chives, divided
- 1 pound fresh lump crabmeat or 3 (6-ounce) cans lump crabmeat, drained and picked over
- ½ cup whole-wheat panko breadcrumbs
- Cooking spray
- 6 large butter lettuce leaves

Directions:
1. Preheat a 6 1/2-quart air fryer to 390°F. Whisk eggs, butter, basil, tarragon, Worcestershire, lemon zest, Old Bay, garlic powder, onion powder, 1/3 cup sour cream and 1 tablespoon chives together in a large bowl. Add crabmeat and panko and stir gently.
2. With clean hands, shape the mixture evenly into 6 crab cakes (1/3 cup each). Generously coat the fry basket with cooking spray. Add 3 crab cakes to the basket; coat the crab cakes with cooking spray. Cook until deeply browned and crispy on both sides, 15 to 18 minutes, turning once and coating with additional cooking spray halfway. Transfer to a plate; cover to keep warm. Repeat with the remaining 3 crab cakes.
3. Place 1 lettuce leaf on each of 6 plates; top each with 1 crab cake. Top each crab cake with about 1 1/2 teaspoons sour cream and 1/2 teaspoon chives. Serve with lemon wedges, if desired.

Nutrition facts:
Calories Per Serving 209; Total Fat: 9g; Sodium: 413mg; Total Carbs:7 g; Fiber: 1g; Protein: 22g

Air-fryer Pistachio-crusted Sea Bass

Servings:4

Ingredients:
- 4 (4-ounce) skin-on black sea bass, halibut or other firm white fish fillets
- ¾ teaspoon kosher salt, divided
- ½ teaspoon ground pepper, divided, plus more for garnish
- ¼ cup whole-milk plain strained yogurt, such as Greek-style
- 2 tablespoons chopped fresh dill or 1 tablespoon dried
- ¼ teaspoon garlic powder
- ¼ cup finely chopped pistachios
- ¼ cup whole-wheat panko breadcrumbs
- 2 tablespoons chopped fresh flat-leaf parsley
- Watercress & extra-virgin olive oil for serving

Directions:
1. Preheat air fryer to 400°F. Coat the air-fryer basket generously with cooking spray.
2. Pat fish dry; arrange, skin-side down, on a baking sheet. Season with 1/2 teaspoon salt and 1/4 teaspoon pepper.
3. Combine yogurt, dill and garlic powder in a small bowl. Brush the mixture on the tops of the fillets.
4. Combine pistachios, panko, parsley and the remaining 1/4 teaspoon each salt and pepper in a shallow dish. Dredge the yogurt-coated sides of the fillets in the panko mixture, pressing to adhere.
5. Arrange the fillets in a single layer, panko-sides up, in the prepared basket. Cook until an instant-read thermometer inserted in the center registers 145°F, 4 to 6 minutes per 1/2-inch thickness of fish.

6. If you like, serve the fish over watercress, drizzle with oil and sprinkle with additional pepper.

Nutrition facts:

Calories Per Serving179; Total Fat: 6g; Sodium: 457mg; Total Carbs: 6g; Fiber: 1g; Sugars:1 g; Protein: 24g

Air-fryer Tilapia

Servings:4

Ingredients:
- Cooking spray
- 1 ¼ pounds tilapia fillets
- 1 teaspoon grated lemon zest
- ¼ teaspoon garlic powder
- ¼ teaspoon onion powder
- ¼ teaspoon salt, divided
- ⅛ teaspoon hot paprika
- ⅛ teaspoon ground white pepper
- 1 tablespoon lemon juice
- 1 teaspoon chopped fresh chives
- 1 teaspoon chopped fresh parsley

Directions:
1. Preheat air fryer to 400°F for 5 minutes. Lightly coat the fryer basket with cooking spray.
2. Pat tilapia fillets dry with paper towels. Coat the fillets with cooking spray.
3. Combine lemon zest, garlic powder, onion powder, 1/8 teaspoon salt, paprika and white pepper in a small bowl. Sprinkle onto the fish.
4. Working in batches if necessary, arrange the fish in a single layer in the fryer basket. Cook, flipping once, until an instant-read thermometer inserted in the center registers 145°F and the fish flakes easily with a fork at the thickest part, 6 to 8 minutes. Drizzle lemon juice over the fillets and sprinkle with the remaining 1/8 teaspoon salt. Sprinkle with chives and parsley before serving.

Nutrition facts:

Calories Per Serving144; Total Fat: 3g; Sodium: 220mg; Total Carbs: 1g; Protein: 29g

Air Fryer Keto Coconut Shrimp

Servings:8

Cooking Time: 10 Minutes

Ingredients:
- 25 large shrimp peeled and deveined
- ½ cup coconut flour
- 1 ¾ cup coconut flakes unsweetened
- 3 eggs
- 1 tablespoon ground black pepper
- 1 teaspoon smoked paprika
- 1 teaspoon salt

Directions:
1. Preheat the Air Fryer to 390 degrees Fahrenheit. Prepare the air fryer basket with non stick cooking spray.
2. Arrange three bowls. Add the coconut flour, paprika, salt and pepper to one bowl. Coconut flakes to the second bowl, and beaten eggs in the third bowl.
3. Dip the shrimp into the coconut flour mixture, then dip into the egg mixture, and finally into the coconut flakes. Set aside on a wire rack until you've finished with all of the shrimp.
4. Add the coconut shrimp in a single layer into the prepared air fryer basket and cook for 8-10 minutes at 380 degrees Fahrenheit. Flip the shrimp halfway through.
5. Remove when golden brown and serve immediately.

Nutrition facts:

Calories Per Serving: 199; Total Fat: 15g; Sodium: 483mg; Total Carbs: 9g; Fiber: 6g; Sugars: 2g; Protein: 8g

Air-fryer Popcorn Shrimp

Servings:4

Ingredients:
- Cooking spray
- ½ cup all-purpose flour
- 2 eggs, well beaten
- 2 tablespoons water
- 1 ½ cups panko breadcrumbs
- 1 tablespoon ground cumin
- 1 tablespoon garlic powder
- 1 pound small shrimp, peeled and deveined
- ½ cup no-salt-added ketchup
- 2 tablespoons chopped chipotle chiles in adobo
- 2 tablespoons chopped fresh cilantro
- 2 tablespoons lime juice
- ⅛ teaspoon kosher salt

Directions:
1. Coat air fryer basket with cooking spray.
2. Place flour in a shallow dish. Combine eggs and water in another shallow dish. Combine panko, cumin and garlic powder in a third shallow dish. Dredge shrimp first in the flour, then in the egg, then in the panko, shaking off excess. Place half of the shrimp in the prepared basket; coat well with cooking spray. Cook at 360°F until crispy and cooked through, about 8 minutes, turning once during cooking. Repeat with the remaining shrimp.
3. Combine ketchup, chipotle chiles, cilantro, lime juice and salt in a small bowl. Serve the dipping sauce with the shrimp.

Nutrition facts:

Calories Per Serving297; Total Fat: 4g; Sodium: 291mg; Total Carbs: 35g; Fiber: 1g; Sugars: 9g; Protein: 29g

Air-fryer Tuna Steak

Servings:4

Ingredients:
- 3 tablespoons lower-sodium tamari or soy sauce
- 1 scallion, thinly sliced
- 1 tablespoon lime juice
- 2 teaspoons sesame oil
- 2 teaspoons honey
- 1 clove garlic, minced
- 2 tablespoons toasted sesame seeds
- 2 (8 ounce) ahi tuna steaks (1 inch thick)

Directions:
1. Combine tamari (or soy sauce), scallion, lime juice, sesame oil, honey and garlic in a small bowl; set aside.
2. Spread sesame seeds on a small plate. Coat both sides of each tuna steak evenly with sesame seeds, pressing to adhere.
3. Preheat air fryer to 375°F. Place the tuna steaks in the fryer basket and cook to desired doneness (about 7 minutes for medium-rare or 10 minutes for medium). Slice the tuna steaks and drizzle evenly with the reserved sauce.

Nutrition facts:
Calories Per Serving 190; Total Fat: 5g; Sodium: 484mg; Total Carbs: 6g; Fiber: 1g; Sugars:3 g; Protein:30 g

Air Fryer Coconut Shrimp

Servings: 4

Cooking Time: 8 Minutes

Ingredients:
- 1 lb large raw shrimp (peeled and deveined)
- (20-30 shrimp
- 2 egg whites (beaten)
- 1 tbsp water
- 1/2 cup whole-wheat panko bread crumbs
- 1/4 cup unsweetened coconut flakes
- 1/2 tsp ground cumin
- 1/2 tsp turmeric
- 1/2 tsp ground coriander
- 1/8 tsp salt
- 1 nonstick cooking spray

Directions:
1. Pat the shrimp dry using paper towels. Place the egg whites and water in a shallow bowl, whisking to combine.
2. Combine the panko bread crumbs, coconut, cumin, turmeric, coriander, and salt in another shallow bowl.
3. Dip the shrimp in the egg mixture, allowing the excess to drip back into the bowl, and then coat in the panko mixture. Place the coated shrimp on a wire rack. Repeat with all shrimp.
4. Place the shrimp in a single layer in the air fryer basket. Spray the shrimp with nonstick cooking spray for 2 seconds. Set the temperature to 400° F and air fry for 4 minutes. Turn the shrimp over. Air fry for 2 to 4 minutes, or until the shrimp are golden brown. Serve warm.

Nutrition facts:
Calories Per Serving 180; Total Fat: 4.5g; Sodium: 230mg; Total Carbs: 9g; Fiber: 2g; Sugars: 1g; Protein: 28g

Air Fryer Scallops Recipe

Servings: 2

Cooking Time: 6 Minutes

Ingredients:
- 1 pound sea scallops
- 1 teaspoon lemon pepper seasoning
- Olive oil spray
- Fresh chopped parsley, to garnish

Directions:
1. Preheat the air fryer to 400°F for 5 minutes.
2. Meanwhile pat dry the scallops with a paper towel, spritz with olive oil and season with lemon pepper seasoning on both sides.
3. Place in the preheated air fryer basket and cook to 400°F for 6 minutes turning halfway through.
4. Remove from the air fryer, serve with your favorite sauce. Enjoy!

Nutrition facts:
Calories Per Serving: 314; Total Fat: 9g; Sodium: 650mg; Total Carbs: 13g; Fiber: 0g; Sugars: 0g; Protein: 47g

Honey Soy-glazed Salmon

Servings: 2

Ingredients:
- 3/4 lbs wild-caught salmon fillet
- 1 Olive oil cooking spray
- 1 Salt and freshly ground pepper
- 1 tbsp honey
- 1 tbsp soy sauce (reduced-sodium)

Directions:

1. Rinse salmon and pat dry with a paper towel.
2. Heat a nonstick skillet over medium-high heat, and spray with olive oil spray.
3. Brown salmon 2 minutes; turn and brown 1 minute. Season the cooked sides with salt and pepper. Lower heat to low, cover, and let cook 7-8 minutes. Remove from heat.
4. Mix honey and soy sauce together. Pour over the salmon, cover, and let sit 1 minute. Serve.

Nutrition facts:

Calories Per Serving 303; Total Fat: 12g; Sodium: 366mg; Total Carbs: 12g; Fiber: 0g; Protein: 39g

Perfect Air Fryr Salmon Fillets

Servings:2
Cooking Time: 15 Minutes

Ingredients:

- 2 4-6 oz salmon fillets
- salt and freshly ground pepper
- 1 lemon
- 1 tbspn chopped fresh dill
- 1 teaspoon lemon juice
- 1/4 cup greek yogurt
- 1/2 teaspoon garlic powder

Directions:

1. Wash and dry your salmon fillets (with paper towels). Slice the lemon and cover the air fryer basket with it
2. Add salt and pepper to the salmon fillet. Place fillets on top of lemons and cook for about 15 minutes at 330 degrees.
3. Meanwhile make the sauce. Mix yogurt with dill and garlic powder. Add lemon juice and salt and pepper if needed.
4. Once the salmon is done, cover it with sauce and serve.

Nutrition facts:

Calories Per Serving: 194; Total Fat: 7g; Sodium: 60mg; Total Carbs: 6g; Fiber: 1g; Sugars: 2g; Protein: 25g

Air-fryer Tuna Patties

Servings:4

Ingredients:

- 2 (5 ounce) cans solid white tuna in water, drained and flaked
- ¾ cup whole-wheat panko
- ¼ cup finely chopped red onion
- ¼ cup finely chopped red bell pepper
- ¼ cup finely chopped celery
- 1 large egg, lightly beaten
- 7 tablespoons mayonnaise, divided
- 3 tablespoons chopped fresh flat-leaf parsley, divided
- 1 ½ teaspoons grated lemon zest, divided
- 2 tablespoons lemon juice, divided
- Cooking spray
- 1 tablespoon Dijon mustard
- 4 cups arugula (about 4 ounces)

Directions:

1. Place tuna, panko, onion, bell pepper, celery, egg, 4 tablespoons mayonnaise, 2 tablespoons parsley, 1 teaspoon lemon zest and 1 tablespoon lemon juice in a medium bowl. Stir gently to combine. Shape the mixture into 8 patties 2 1/2 inches in diameter and about 1/2 inch thick (about 1/3 cup mixture per patty). Place the patties on a parchment-paper-lined plate and refrigerate for 20 minutes.

2. Meanwhile, preheat an air fryer to 360°F for 15 minutes. Lightly coat the fry basket with cooking spray and coat each patty with cooking spray. Working in batches if needed, add the patties to the basket in a single layer; cook until slightly crisp and heated through, about 6 minutes per side. (Lightly coat the basket with cooking spray between batches.)
3. Meanwhile, combine mustard and the remaining 3 tablespoons mayonnaise, 1 tablespoon parsley, 1/2 teaspoon lemon zest and 1 tablespoon lemon juice in a small bowl; stir until smooth. Place 2 tuna patties, 1 cup arugula and 1 tablespoon mayonnaise sauce on each of 4 plates.

Nutrition facts:

Calories Per Serving335; Total Fat: 22g; Sodium: 470mg; Total Carbs: 14g; Fiber: 3g; Sugars: 2g; Protein: 22g

Air-fryer Beer-battered Fish

Servings:4

Ingredients:

- 1 ¼ pounds skinless cod fillet, about 1 inch thick, cut into 8 portions
- 1 ¾ cups all-purpose flour, divided
- 1 ½ teaspoons garlic powder
- 1 ½ teaspoons paprika
- Pinch of cayenne pepper
- ½ teaspoon salt, divided
- ¼ teaspoon ground pepper
- ½ teaspoon baking soda
- ¾ cup beer, preferably lager
- 1 large egg, lightly beaten

Directions:

1. Pat fish dry; refrigerate while making batter.
2. Whisk 3/4 cup flour, garlic powder, paprika, cayenne, 1/4 teaspoon salt and pepper in a shallow dish; set aside. Whisk the remaining 1 cup flour and baking soda in a medium bowl. Add beer and egg and whisk until smooth (the batter should be thick). Refrigerate the batter.
3. Preheat air fryer to 390°F (see Tip). Coat the basket generously with cooking spray. Remove the fish and batter from the refrigerator and set a large rimmed baking sheet on the counter. Pat the fish dry again. Lightly dredge each piece of fish in the flour-spice mixture, tapping off excess, and transfer to one half of the baking sheet. Spread the remaining flour-spice mixture on the other half of the baking sheet.
4. Using 2 forks, dip a piece of fish into the batter, letting excess batter drip off, then place in the flour-spice mixture, gently flipping until well coated. Repeat with the remaining fish. Once all the fish is coated, spray the top side with cooking spray until no dry flour remains. Arrange the fish pieces sprayed-side down in the air-fryer basket, without touching. Generously spray the tops and sides of the fish with cooking spray. Cook until the coating is golden brown and the fish flakes easily with a fork, about 13 minutes. Gently remove the fish with a flexible spatula (some batter may stick to the bottom of the basket). Sprinkle with the remaining 1/4 teaspoon salt and serve immediately.

Nutrition facts:

Calories Per Serving338; Total Fat:5 g; Sodium: 484mg; Total Carbs:37 g; Fiber: 2g; Protein: 31g

Air-fryer Scallops

Servings: 2

Ingredients:
- 8 large (1-oz.) sea scallops, cleaned and patted very dry
- ¼ teaspoon ground pepper
- ⅛ teaspoon salt
- Cooking spray
- ¼ cup extra-virgin olive oil
- 2 tablespoons very finely chopped flat-leaf parsley
- 2 teaspoons very finely chopped capers
- 1 teaspoon finely grated lemon zest
- ½ teaspoon finely chopped garlic

Directions:
1. Sprinkle scallops with pepper and salt. Coat the basket of an air fryer with cooking spray. Place scallops in the basket and coat them with cooking spray. Place the basket in the fryer. Cook the scallops at 400°F until they reach an internal temperature of 120°F, about 6 minutes.
2. Combine oil, parsley, capers, lemon zest and garlic in a small bowl. Drizzle over the scallops.

Nutrition facts:
Calories Per Serving 348; Total Fat: 30g; Sodium: 660mg; Total Carbs: 5g; Fiber: 0g; Sugars: 0g; Protein: 14g

Air-fryer Coconut Shrimp

Servings: 8

Ingredients:
- ⅓ cup granulated sugar
- ⅓ cup rice vinegar
- 2 tablespoons chile-garlic sauce
- ½ cup water plus 2 tablespoons, divided
- 1 teaspoon salt, divided
- 1 tablespoon cornstarch
- ½ cup all-purpose flour
- 1 teaspoon garlic powder
- 2 large egg whites
- 1 cup unsweetened shredded coconut
- ½ cup whole-wheat panko breadcrumbs
- 24 large raw shrimp, peeled and deveined, tails left on
- Cooking spray

Directions:
1. Combine sugar, vinegar, chile-garlic sauce, 1/2 cup water and 1/2 teaspoon salt in a small saucepan. Bring the mixture a boil over high heat; cook, stirring occasionally, until reduced slightly, about 5 minutes. Stir cornstarch and the remaining 2 tablespoons water together in a small bowl. Add to the mixture in the saucepan; cook, stirring occasionally, until bubbling and thickened, about 30 seconds. Remove the sauce from the heat and set aside.
2. Preheat air fryer to 400°F. Combine flour, garlic powder and the remaining 1/2 teaspoon salt in a shallow dish. Place egg whites in a separate shallow dish and whisk until frothy. Stir coconut and panko together in a third shallow dish. Dredge shrimp in the flour mixture and then dredge in the egg whites,

shaking off excess; dredge in the coconut mixture, pressing to adhere.

3. Arrange half the shrimp in an even layer in the fryer basket; coat the shrimp well with cooking spray. Cook until crispy and golden, about 6 minutes. Transfer to a plate. Repeat the procedure with the remaining shrimp. Serve with the sauce.

Nutrition facts:

Calories Per Serving164; Total Fat: 6g; Sodium: 476mg; Total Carbs: 17g; Fiber: 2g; Sugars: 8g; Protein: 11g

Crab Stuffed Shrimp

Servings:4

Cooking Time: 10 Minutes

Ingredients:
- 4 oz drained, canned lump crab meat
- 2 tbsp finely chopped green onions
- 1 tbsp light mayonnaise
- 2 tbsp lemon zest
- 1 tsp Fresno pepper (very finely chopped)
- 1 1/2 tbsp whole wheat panko (Japanese bread crumbs)
- 12 extra large (about 21–25 count) shrimp
- 1 Extra virgin olive oil pan spray

Directions:
1. Preheat the oven to 475°F. Line a small baking sheet with nonstick foil.
2. Mix the crab, green onions, mayonnaise, lemon zest, and peppers in small bowl until they are well combined.
3. Spread the bread crumbs on a small plate and set aside.
4. To butterfly the shrimp: Peel all but the tail and last joint of the shell off the shrimp. On a cutting board, place a shrimp so that the head end and tail are touching the cutting board and the center arches toward the ceiling. Insert a knife into the shrimp near the head, just past the remaining shell, and cut down the center of the shrimp's back to the tail, cutting just deep enough to flatten the shrimp (make sure not to cut all the way through). Run the shrimp under cold water to clean it. Dry it well with paper towels. Repeat the procedure with the remaining shrimp and place them side by side, not touching, on the prepared baking sheet.
5. Divide the crab mixture evenly among the shrimp, about 1/2 tablespoon per shrimp, forming it into a tight mound on top of the butterflied portion of each shrimp.
6. Carefully dip each shrimp, gently turning it upside down, into the bread crumbs to lightly coat the crab (not the whole shrimp, just the portion with the crab). Return shrimp to the baking sheet and make sure the crab mound isn't flattened (if it is, reshape it slightly to look like a mound). Sprinkle any remaining bread crumbs evenly over the tops. Mist the tops lightly with spray.
7. Bake the shrimp 7–10 minutes or until they are no longer translucent throughout. Enjoy immediately.

Nutrition facts:

Calories Per Serving 80; Total Fat: 1.5g; Sodium: 220mg; Total Carbs: 3g; Fiber: 0g; Sugars: 0g; Protein: 14g

Asian Tuna Salad

Servings: 4

Ingredients:
- 2 tbsp light or reduced sodium soy sauce
- 1 1/2 tbsp Splenda® Brown Sugar Blend
- 1 tsp Asian Hot Sauce (Siracha, optional)
- 1/4 tsp black pepper
- 1 nonstick cooking spray
- 1 lbs fresh albacore tuna
- 1 lbs asparagus (trimmed)
- 1 tsp sesame seeds
- 6 cup mixed baby lettuces or mesclun mix (washed and dried (or spun in a salad spinner))
- 1 large red bell pepper (julienned)
- 1 medium cucumber (seeded and julienned)
- 1/4 cup rice wine vinegar
- 1 tbsp Splenda® Brown Sugar Blend
- 1 tbsp toasted sesame oil
- 1/8 tsp black pepper

Directions:
1. Preheat an indoor or outdoor grill.
2. In a small bowl, whisk together the soy sauce, Splenda Brown Sugar, hot sauce (optional) and black pepper. Set aside.
3. Spray the indoor grill with cooking spray. Or, if using an outdoor grill ensure the grates are cleaned and lightly oiled.
4. Brush tuna and asparagus with the soy sauce marinade. Place onto grill. Grill the tuna for 3 minutes on each side. Grill asparagus, turning often, until beginning to soften (about 6-8 minutes). Remove tuna and asparagus from grill, sprinkle with sesame seeds and set aside to cool. Tuna should be slightly pink in the center but not raw.
5. Toss the lettuce, red bell pepper and cucumber in a salad bowl.
6. In a small bowl whisk dressing ingredients. Pour over salad and toss gently to coat. Divide the salad equally among four plates.
7. Once tuna and asparagus are cool to room temperature or slightly warmer, slice the tuna and divide equally among the four salads (just under 4 ounces of tuna per salad). Lay it gently on top of the salad.
8. Cut the asparagus spears in half and lay them around the edge of the salad.

Nutrition facts:
Calories Per Serving 265; Total Fat: 6g; Sodium: 350mg; Total Carbs: 18g; Fiber: 4g; Protein: 34g

Air-fryer Salmon With Horseradish Rub

Servings: 2

Ingredients:
- Cooking spray
- 2 tablespoons finely grated horseradish
- 1 tablespoon finely chopped flat-leaf parsley
- 1 tablespoon capers, finely chopped
- 1 tablespoon extra-virgin olive oil
- 1 (12 ounce) skinless salmon fillet (about 1 inch thick)
- ¼ teaspoon salt
- ¼ teaspoon ground pepper

Directions:
1. Coat the basket of an air fryer with cooking spray.
2. Combine horseradish, parsley, capers and oil in a small bowl. Sprinkle salmon with salt and pepper. Spread the horseradish mixture over the top of the salmon. Coat with cooking spray.

3. Place the salmon in the prepared basket. Cook at 375 degrees F until internal temperature registers 130 degrees F, about 15 minutes. Let rest for 5 minutes before serving.

Nutrition facts:

Calories Per Serving 284; Total Fat:14 g; Sodium: 540mg; Total Carbs: 3g; Fiber: 1g; Sugars: 1g; Protein: 34g

Instant Pot Panko-crusted Cod

Servings:4

Cooking Time: 8 Minutes

Ingredients:

- 1/2 cup panko bread crumbs
- 2 tbsp olive oil
- 2 tsp lemon zest
- 1/4 tsp salt
- 1/4 cup light mayonnaise
- 2 tsp lemon juice
- 1/2 tsp dried thyme
- 4 (6-oz) fillets cod or other white fish
- 1 cup water
- 1 lemon (cut into 4 wedges)

Directions:

1. Press the Sauté button, then press the Adjust button to "More" or "High." When the display says "Hot," add the bread crumbs and cook for 2 minutes, or until golden brown, stirring frequently. Stir in the oil, lemon zest, and salt. Remove from the pot and set aside on a plate.
2. In a small bowl, combine the mayonnaise, lemon juice, and thyme. Spread equal amounts over the top of each cod fillet.
3. Place the water and a steamer basket in the Instant Pot. Add the fish to the steamer basket, mayonnaise side up. Seal the lid, close the valve, press the Cancel button, and set to Manual/Pressure Cook for 3 minutes.
4. Use a quick pressure release. When the valve drops, carefully remove the lid. Remove the steamer basket and fish from the pot. Serve the fish topped with the bread crumb mixture. Serve with the lemon wedges to squeeze over all.

Nutrition facts:

Calories Per Serving 270; Total Fat: 0g; Sodium:370mg; Total Carbs: 10g; Fiber: 1g; Sugars: 2g; Protein: 31g

Fried Shrimp

Servings:2

Cooking Time: 20 Minutes

Ingredients:

- 2 pounds large shrimp
- 1 teaspoon garlic powder
- 1 large egg
- 1 tsp, ground pepper
- 1 teaspoon salt
- 1 cup of finely crushed pork rinds (they should be like bread crumbs).

Directions:

1. In a bowl, mix together your salt, garlic powder, and crushed pork rinds.
2. In a separte bowl, beat your egg and add your ground pepper.
3. Dip your shrimp in the egg, and then in the pork rind and spice mixture. You can do this multiple times to make sure it's well-coated on all sides.
4. Spray the tray of your air fryer with non-stick spray and add your shrimp in an even layer.

5. Cook according to the specifications of your air fryer. My Gourmia Air Fryer took 20 minutes at 325 degrees. You can check yours halfway through. Measure that the internal temp reads 145 degrees.
6. Eat with chilli sauce, or spritz with lemon and sriracha. Plate and enjoy.

Nutrition facts:
Calories Per Serving: 367; Total Fat: 21.4g; Sodium: 1667.8mg; Total Carbs: 1.2g; Fiber: 3g; Sugars: 0.2g; Protein: 39.7g

Air Fryer Shrimp Recipe

Servings:4
Cooking Time: 10 Minutes

Ingredients:
- 1 pound large raw shrimp, peeled and deveined
- 1 teaspoon minced garlic
- 1 tablespoon unsalted melted butter
- 1 teaspoon lemon juice
- Salt and pepper to taste (optional)
- Chopped parsley to garnish

Directions:
1. Preheat air fryer to 350°F for 4 minutes
2. In a medium bowl add the shrimp, garlic, butter, and lemon juice; toss gently to coat evenly.
3. Place the shrimp inside the air fryer basket and cook for 8 to 10 minutes depending on the size of the shrimp, shaking the basket or stirring halfway through.
4. Remove the shrimp from the air fryer, sprinkle with fresh parsley and wedges of lemon. Enjoy!

Nutrition facts:
Calories Per Serving: 108; Total Fat: 4g; Sodium: 739mg; Total Carbs: 1g; Fiber: 0g; Sugars: 0g; Protein: 16g

Teriyaki Salmon Air Fryer

Servings:4
Cooking Time: 10 Minutes

Ingredients:
- For the teriyaki sauce
- 1/2 cup reduced sodium soy sauce
- 1/4 cup mirin (sweetened sake)
- 2 tablespoons dark brown sugar
- 1/2 teaspoon toasted sesame oil
- 2 cloves garlic minced
- 1 1 inch finger ginger minced, about 1 tablespoon
- Salmon
- 1 1/2 pounds salmon filet skin on, cut into 4 equal sized pieces
- For serving
- Black sesame seeds
- Lime wedges

Directions:
1. Make the teriyaki sauce, by whisking together soy sauce, mirin, brown sugar, sesame oil, ginger and garlic in a small saucepan over medium heat. Bring to a boil, then reduce to a simmer. Simmer for 5 minutes, then remove from heat. Cool slightly.
2. Add ¾ of the sauce to a sealable zip lock bag. Add the salmon and make sure the filets are covered in marinade. Set aside for 30 minutes at room temperature.
3. Pour the remaining ¼ of the sauce into a small serving bowl. You will use this later to serve with the salmon as a dipping sauce.
4. Preheat your air fryer to 390 degrees.
5. Wipe or spray your air fryer basket with avocado oil or other high heat cooking oil.
6. Remove salmon from teriyaki marinade (discard remaining marinade), shaking off excess marinade,

and place salmon in the air fryer, spacing the filets out so they don't touch each other.
7. Cook salmon for 5-6 minutes, or until desired doneness - time will vary depending on the thickness of your salmon filets and the variation in air fryers. Salmon is cooked through at an internal temperature of 145 degrees, but keep in mind, the fish will continue cooking at least an additional 5 degrees once you remove it from the air fryer, so best to pull it out at about 140 degrees (or less if you prefer it medium).
8. Plate salmon. Sprinkle with black sesame seeds and serve with lime wedges. Serve with reserved teriyaki sauce.

Nutrition facts:

Calories Per Serving: 310; Total Fat: 11g; Sodium: 1252mg; Total Carbs: 15g; Fiber: 1g; Sugars: 10g; Protein: 36g

Air-fryer Fish Tacos

Servings:4

Ingredients:

- 2 cups shredded green cabbage
- ¼ cup coarsely chopped fresh cilantro
- 1 scallion, thinly sliced
- 5 tablespoons lime juice (from 2 limes), divided
- 1 tablespoon avocado oil
- 1 large avocado
- 2 tablespoons sour cream
- 1 small clove garlic, grated
- ¼ teaspoon salt
- 1 large egg white
- ⅓ cup dry whole-wheat breadcrumbs
- 1 tablespoon chili powder
- 1 pound skinless mahi-mahi fillets, cut into 2- to 3-inch strips
- Avocado oil cooking spray
- 8 (6 inch) corn tortillas, warmed
- 1 medium tomato, chopped

Directions:

1. Toss cabbage, cilantro, scallion, 2 tablespoons lime juice and avocado oil together in a medium bowl; set aside.
2. Cut avocado in half lengthwise; using a spoon, scoop the pulp into the bowl of a mini food processor. Add sour cream, garlic, salt and the remaining 3 tablespoons lime juice; process until smooth, about 30 seconds. (Alternatively, mash with a fork to reach desired consistency.) Set aside.
3. Preheat air fryer to 400°F. Place egg white in a shallow dish; whisk until frothy. Combine breadcrumbs and chili powder in a separate shallow dish. Pat fish dry with a paper towel. Coat the fish with egg white, letting excess drip off; dredge in the breadcrumb mixture, pressing to adhere.
4. Working in batches if needed, arrange the fish in an even layer in the fryer basket; coat the fish well with cooking spray. Cook until crispy and golden on one side, about 3 minutes. Flip the fish; coat with cooking spray and cook until it's crispy and flakes easily, about 3 minutes. Flake the fish into bite-size pieces. Top each tortilla evenly with fish, avocado crema (about 1 tablespoon each), cabbage slaw (about 1/4 cup each) and tomato. Serve with lime wedges, if desired.

Nutrition facts:

Calories Per Serving377; Total Fat: 15g; Sodium: 341mg; Total Carbs: 36g; Fiber: 8g; Sugars: 3g; Protein:27 g

Air-fryer Shrimp

Servings:4

Ingredients:
- 1 pound peeled and deveined large shrimp, tails on
- 2 tablespoons extra-virgin olive oil
- 2 tablespoons lemon juice
- 2 cloves garlic, grated
- ½ teaspoon crushed red pepper, plus more for garnish
- ¼ teaspoon salt
- 1 tablespoon minced fresh chives

Directions:
1. Preheat air fryer to 400°F. Combine shrimp, oil, lemon juice, garlic, crushed red pepper and salt in a medium bowl; toss to mix well.
2. Transfer the shrimp to the fryer basket with a slotted spoon. Cook until the shrimp turn pink and opaque, about 5 minutes. Transfer to a serving dish; sprinkle with chives and additional crushed red pepper, if desired. Serve with lemon wedges.

Nutrition facts:
Calories Per Serving164; Total Fat: 8g; Sodium: 281mg; Total Carbs: 1g; Protein: 23g

Air-fryer Salmon Cakes

Servings:2

Ingredients:
- Cooking spray
- 2 7.5-ounce cans unsalted pink salmon (with skin and bones)
- 1 large egg
- ½ cup whole-wheat panko breadcrumbs
- 2 tablespoons chopped fresh dill
- 2 tablespoons canola mayonnaise
- 2 teaspoons Dijon mustard
- ¼ teaspoon ground pepper
- 2 lemon wedges

Directions:
1. Coat the basket of an air fryer with cooking spray.
2. Drain salmon; remove and discard any large bones and skin. Place the salmon in a medium bowl. Add egg, panko, dill, mayonnaise, mustard and pepper; stir gently until combined. Shape the mixture into 4 3-inch-diameter cakes.
3. Coat the cakes with cooking spray; place them in the prepared basket. Cook at 400°F until browned and an instant-read thermometer inserted into the thickest portion registers 160°F, about 12 minutes. Serve with lemon wedges.

Nutrition facts:
Calories Per Serving517; Total Fat: 27g; Sodium: 384mg; Total Carbs: 15g; Fiber: 2g; Sugars: 1g; Protein:52 g

Air-fryer Fish Cakes

Servings:2

Ingredients:
- Cooking spray
- 10 ounces finely chopped white fish (such as grouper, catfish or cod)
- ⅔ cup whole-wheat panko breadcrumbs
- 3 tablespoons finely chopped fresh cilantro
- 2 tablespoons Thai sweet chili sauce
- 2 tablespoons canola mayonnaise
- 1 large egg
- ⅛ teaspoon salt
- ¼ teaspoon ground pepper
- 2 lime wedges

Directions:

1. Coat the basket of an air fryer with cooking spray.
2. Combine fish, panko, cilantro, chili sauce, mayonnaise, egg, salt and pepper in a medium bowl; stir until well combined. Shape the mixture into four 3-inch-diameter cakes.
3. Coat the cakes with cooking spray; place in the prepared basket. Cook at 400 degrees F until the cakes are browned and their internal temperature reaches 140 degrees F, 9 to 10 minutes. Serve with lime wedges.

Nutrition facts:

Calories Per Serving 399; Total Fat: 16g; Sodium: 537mg; Total Carbs: 28g; Fiber: 3g; Sugars: 5g; Protein: 35g

Air-fryer Salmon

Servings: 2

Ingredients:
- 3 medium cloves garlic
- ¼ teaspoon kosher salt
- 1 teaspoon grated lemon zest
- 2 tablespoons lemon juice
- 1 tablespoon extra-virgin olive oil
- ¼ teaspoon ground coriander
- ½ teaspoon Aleppo pepper or chili powder, divided
- 2 (6 ounce) skin-on salmon fillets
- 1 tablespoon chopped fresh flat-leaf parsley
- Lemon wedges for serving

Directions:
1. Preheat air fryer to 375°F for 15 minutes. Meanwhile, finely chop garlic. Add salt to the garlic on a cutting board; chop and mash the mixture together with the flat side of a knife to form a paste. Transfer to a small bowl.
2. Add lemon juice, oil, coriander and 1/4 teaspoon Aleppo pepper (or chili powder) to the garlic mixture; whisk to combine. Pat salmon dry; spoon the mixture evenly over the tops of the fillets.
3. Coat the basket of the air fryer with cooking spray; arrange the salmon, skin-side down, in the basket. Cook until browned and just cooked through, about 12 minutes. Remove from the air fryer.
4. Top the salmon evenly with lemon zest, parsley and the remaining 1/4 teaspoon Aleppo pepper (or chili powder). Serve immediately, with lemon wedges if desired.

Nutrition facts:

Calories Per Serving 315; Total Fat: 18g; Sodium: 336mg; Total Carbs: 3g; Fiber: 1g; Sugars: 1g; Protein: 34g

BEEF, PORK AND LAMB RECIPES

Classic Beef Stew

Servings: 10

Cooking Time: 2 Hours

Ingredients:
- 2 tbsp all-purpose flour or whole-wheat pastry flour
- 1 tbsp Italian seasoning
- 3 tbsp olive oil
- 2 lbs top round (cut into 3/4-inch cubes)
- 1 1/2 lbs cremini (baby bella) mushrooms (cleaned, stemmed, and quartered)
- 4 cup low sodium chicken broth (reduced-sodium, low-fat, divided use)
- 1 large onion (coarsely chopped)
- 3 clove garlic (minced)
- 2 large russet potatoes
- 3 medium carrots (peeled)
- 1 cup frozen peas
- 1 tbsp fresh thyme (minced)
- 1 tbsp red wine vinegar
- 1/2 tsp freshly ground black pepper (1/4-1/2 tsp)

Directions:
1. Combine the all-purpose flour with the Italian seasoning. Heat the olive oil in a large Dutch oven over medium heat. Dredge the beef cubes lightly in the flour mixture and add the beef, in batches to keep the beef in one layer, until well browned on each side.
2. Remove the beef from the pan and deglaze the pan with 1/4 cup chicken broth. Add in the mushrooms and sauté for about 4 minutes until well browned. Remove the mushrooms from the pan and deglaze with another 1/4 cup of the broth. Add the onions and garlic and sauté for 4 minutes. Return the beef to the pot, add the remaining chicken broth, and bring to a boil. Partially cover, lower the heat to simmer, and cook for 45 minutes, stirring occasionally.
3. Peel and cut the potatoes into 3/4-inch pieces. Cut the carrots into 1/2-inch pieces. Add the potatoes and carrots to the stew and continue to cook for another 45 minutes or until vegetables are tender. Add in the reserved mushrooms, peas, and thyme. Season with red wine vinegar and black pepper.

Nutrition facts:
Calories Per Serving 250; Total Fat: 7g; Sodium: 290mg; Total Carbs: 24g; Fiber: 3g; Sugars: 5g; Protein: 25g

Tuscan-spiced Pork & Mashed Potatoes With Green Beans And Roasted Tomato Dressing

Servings: 2

Cooking Time: 25 Minutes

Ingredients:
- 3/4 lbs golden potatoes
- 2 clove garlic
- 6 oz fresh green beans
- 2 tbsp sliced almonds
- 1 tbsp red wine vinegar
- 4 1/2 tsp olive oil (divided use)
- 1 tsp ground fennel
- 1 tsp fennel seeds

- 1/2 tsp ground rosemary
- 1/2 tsp ground sage
- 1/3 cup low sodium chicken broth
- 2 (6 oz each) boneless pork cutlets

Directions:

1. Prepare the ingredients & start the dressing: Place an oven rack in the center of the oven, then preheat to 450°F. Fill a medium pot 3/4 of the way up with water; cover and heat to boiling on high. Wash and dry the fresh produce. Medium dice the potatoes. Peel 2 cloves of garlic. Using a zester, finely grate 1 clove into a paste (or use the small side of a box grater). Using the flat side of your knife, smash the remaining clove once. Cut off and discard the stem ends of the green beans. Roughly chop the almonds. In a large bowl, combine the chopped almonds, vinegar, 2 teaspoons of olive oil, and as much of the garlic paste as you'd like; season with salt (optional) and pepper. Combine the ground fennel, fennel seeds, ground rosemary, and ground sage in a small bowl.
2. Cook & mash the potatoes: Add the diced potatoes and smashed garlic clove to the pot of boiling water. Cook 16 to 18 minutes, or until tender when pierced with a fork. Turn off the heat. Drain thoroughly and return to the pot. Add the broth. Using a fork or potato masher, mash to your desired consistency. Taste, then season with salt and pepper if desired. Cover to keep warm.
3. Roast the vegetables: Meanwhile, place the prepared green beans on a sheet pan; drizzle with 1 teaspoon of olive oil and season with salt (optional) and pepper. Toss to coat. Arrange in an even layer on one side of the sheet pan. Place the tomatoes on the other side of the sheet pan. Drizzle with 1/2 teaspoon of olive oil and season with salt (optional) and pepper. Toss to coat. Roast 10 to 12 minutes, or until browned and tender when pierced with a fork. Remove from the oven.
4. Cook the pork: Meanwhile, pat the pork dry with paper towels; season on both sides with pepper and enough of the spice blend to coat (you may have extra). In a medium pan (nonstick, if you have one), heat 1 teaspoon of olive oil on medium-high until hot. Add the seasoned pork. Cook 2 to 3 minutes per side, or until browned and cooked through.* Transfer to a plate and let rest at least 5 minutes.
5. * An instant-read thermometer should register 145°F.
6. Dress the green beans & serve your dish: While the pork rests, carefully transfer the roasted tomatoes to the bowl of dressing. Using a fork, smash the tomatoes to release their liquid. Stir to combine. Add the roasted green beans and stir to coat. Serve the rested pork with the mashed potatoes and dressed green beans.

Nutrition facts:

Calories Per Serving 440; Total Fat: 18g; Sodium: 190mg; Total Carbs: 43g; Fiber: 9g; Sugars: 6g; Protein: 31g

Air-fryer Pork Chops

Servings:2

Ingredients:

- ½ cup panko breadcrumbs
- 1 teaspoon paprika
- ¼ teaspoon garlic powder
- ¼ teaspoon onion powder
- 2 (5 ounce) boneless pork chops, trimmed
- Cooking spray
- ¼ teaspoon salt

Directions:

1. Place panko, paprika, garlic powder and onion powder in a large zip-top plastic bag. Add pork; seal the bag and shake to coat. Remove the pork from the bag; shake off excess breading. Place the pork in air-fryer basket; coat with cooking spray. Cook at 360°F until the pork is browned and an instant-read thermometer inserted in the thickest part registers 145°F, 15 to 17 minutes. Transfer the pork to a plate; let rest for 5 minutes. Sprinkle evenly with salt.

Nutrition facts:

Calories Per Serving 230; Total Fat: 6g; Sodium: 372mg; Total Carbs: 16g; Fiber: 1g; Sugars: 1g; Protein: 25g

Air-fryer Pork Tenderloin

Servings: 4

Ingredients:

- 1 tablespoon brown sugar
- 2 teaspoons Dijon mustard
- 1 teaspoon balsamic vinegar
- ½ teaspoon garlic powder
- ½ teaspoon onion powder
- ½ teaspoon smoked paprika
- ½ teaspoon salt
- ¼ teaspoon ground pepper
- 1 pound pork tenderloin, trimmed

Directions:

1. Preheat air fryer to 400°F for 5 minutes.
2. Whisk brown sugar, mustard, vinegar, garlic powder, onion powder, paprika, salt and pepper together in a small bowl.
3. Pat pork dry with paper towels. (If using a small air fryer, cut the pork in half crosswise.) Rub the spice mixture onto the pork and place in the fryer basket. Cook until an instant-read thermometer inserted in the thickest part registers 145°F, 15 to 18 minutes. Let rest for 5 minutes before slicing.

Nutrition facts:

Calories Per Serving 144; Total Fat: 3 g; Sodium: 413mg; Total Carbs: 4g; Sugars: 3g; Protein: 24g

Air Fryer Steak

Servings: 1
Cooking Time: 7 Minutes

Ingredients:

- 8 oz New York Strip steak
- Air Fryer Steak Marinade
- 3 tbsp coconut aminos 45mls
- 3 tbsp lime juice 45mls
- 1 tbsp olive oil
- 1/2 tsp cumin omit for AIP
- 1 clove garlic

Directions:

1. Add the marinade ingredients together and whisk to combine.
2. Place the steak in a non reactive container where it can be covered by the marinade at least half way up the side of the steak. Marinate the steak covered for 15 minutes at room temperature, then turn the steak over and marinade for 15 more minutes.
3. Preheat your Air fryer to 400°F (200°C)
4. Place the steak inside the air fryer basket and cook for about 3 minutes for medium rare, then turn the steak and cook for 4 minutes longer if you like your steak cooked well done.
5. All Air Fryers are different so the exact timing may vary.

6. Once cooked remove and let it rest for ten minutes before slicing.

Nutrition facts:

Calories Per Serving: 696; Total Fat: 48g; Sodium: 1138mg; Total Carbs: 14g; Fiber: 0g; Sugars: 1g; Protein: 47g

Bulgogi

Servings:4
Cooking Time: 10 Minutes

Ingredients:

- 1/2 tsp black pepper
- 1 tbsp honey or 2 packets artificial sweetener
- 3 tbsp lower sodium soy sauce
- 2 tbsp water
- 2 tsp rice wine vinegar
- 1 (16-oz) bag frozen stir-fry vegetables
- 2 clove garlic (picado)
- 3 green onion (scallion) ((partes blancas y verdes), picado)
- 12 oz lean boneless beef tenderloin

Directions:

1. Wrap the meat in plastic and freeze until firm (but not as hard as a stone). Once firm, cut the meat into long and thin strips. Put it in the oven.
2. In a small bowl, stir the onions, garlic, yellow wine vinegar, water, soy sauce, pepper, and pepper. Pour the mixture onto the meat and let it marinate in the refrigerator for at least 30 minutes and at most 2 hours. When the meat is marinated, preheat it using an internal or external grill.
3. Remove the meat from the marinade and shake any excess. Roast the meat on each side for 2-3 minutes or cook until cooked.
4. He steamed vegetables and placed meat on them.

Nutrition facts:

Calories Per Serving 180; Total Fat: 4.5g; Sodium: 200mg; Total Carbs: 13g; Fiber: 3g; Sugars: 6g; Protein: 0g

Air-fryer Steak Fajitas

Servings:6

Ingredients:

- 2 large tomatoes, seeded and chopped
- 1/2 cup diced red onion
- 1/4 cup lime juice
- 1 jalapeno pepper, seeded and minced
- 3 tablespoons minced fresh cilantro
- 2 teaspoons ground cumin, divided
- 3/4 teaspoon salt, divided
- 1 beef flank steak (about 1-1/2 pounds)
- 1 large onion, halved and sliced
- 6 whole wheat tortillas (8 inches), warmed
- Optional: Sliced avocado and lime wedges

Directions:

1. For salsa, place first 5 ingredients in a small bowl; stir in 1 teaspoon cumin and 1/4 teaspoon salt. Let stand until serving.
2. Preheat air fryer to 400°. Sprinkle steak with the remaining cumin and salt. Place on greased tray in air-fryer basket. Cook until meat reaches desired doneness (for medium-rare, a thermometer should read 135°; medium, 140°; medium-well, 145°), 6-8 minutes per side. Remove from basket and let stand 5 minutes.
3. Meanwhile, place onion on tray in air-fryer basket. Cook until crisp-tender, 2-3 minutes, stirring once. Slice steak thinly across the grain; serve in tortillas with onion and salsa. If desired, serve with avocado and lime wedges.

Nutrition facts:

Calories Per Serving: 138; Total Fat: 1.3g; Sodium: 426mg; Total Carbs: 28.1g; Fiber: 4.7g; Sugars: 3.2g; Protein: 5.1g

Air Fryer Jalepeno Poppers

Servings:6

Cooking Time: 12 Minutes

Ingredients:
- 6 medium Jalapeños
- 4 ounces cream cheese, softened
- 6-12 slices bacon

Directions:
1. Cut the jalapeños in half, lengthwise. Remove all of the seeds and rinse the jalapeños.
2. Cut small slices of the cream cheese, in strips, and place a strip inside each half piece of the pepper.
3. Wrap a piece of bacon around the stuffed pepper and secure with a toothpick.
4. Place the stuffed peppers in the basket of the air fryer, working in batches if necessary. Be sure they aren't overlapping each other in the basket.
5. Cook at 370 degrees Fahrenheit for 10-12 minutes, until the bacon is cooked to your desired crispness.

Nutrition facts:

Calories Per Serving: 78; Total Fat: 8g; Sodium: 63mg; Total Carbs: 2g; Fiber: 1g; Sugars: 1g; Protein: 1g

Ham And Edamame Chop Salad

Servings:4

Ingredients:
- 1/4 cup light mayonnaise
- 1/3 cup sour cream (fat-free)
- 1 clove medium garlic (minced)
- 2 cider vinegar
- 1 tbsp dried dill (dried)
- 6 cup romaine lettuce (chopped)
- 1 cup fresh shelled edamame
- 4 oz extra-lean ham (diced)
- 1/2 medium cucumber (peeled and chopped)
- 1/2 cup green bell pepper (diced)
- 1/3 cup red onion (diced)
- 2 oz Swiss cheese (very thinly sliced, reduced-fat, torn in small pieces)
- 2 large hard boiled eggs (peeled and halved)

Directions:
1. In a small bowl, stir together the dressing ingredients.
2. In a large bowl, combine the salad ingredients, except the eggs. Cut the eggs in half, discard two yolk halves, and chop the remaining eggs. Add eggs to the salad with the dressing and toss until well coated.

Nutrition facts:

Calories Per Serving 200; Total Fat: 9g; Sodium: 530mg; Total Carbs:15g; Fiber: 4g; Sugars: 5g; Protein: 17g

Beef Fajitas

Servings: 4

Cooking Time: 10 Minutes

Ingredients:
- 2 tsp canola oil
- 2 cup sliced onion
- 2 cup sliced bell peppers
- 20 oz cooked sliced steak from Coffee-Rubbed Steak recipe
- 1/4 tsp salt
- 4 (8-inch) whole wheat flour tortillas

Directions:
1. Heat the oil in a large nonstick skillet over medium-high heat. Add the onion and bell pepper. Sauté for 5 minutes. Add the cooked sliced steak and sauté for 2 to 3 minutes to warm. Sprinkle with salt.
2. Wrap the tortillas in damp paper towels and microwave on high for 1 minute.
3. Place each tortilla on a plate. Divide the steak, onions, and peppers among the 4 tortillas. Wrap and serve. These fajitas go well with a green salad.

Nutrition facts:

Calories Per Serving 470; Total Fat: 18g; Sodium: 510mg; Total Carbs: 31g; Fiber: 5g; Sugars: 4g; Protein: 45g

Asian Pork Chops

Servings: 4

Cooking Time: 10 Minutes

Ingredients:
- 2 tablespoons plus 1 teaspoon soy sauce (reduced-sodium)
- 3 tbsp rice wine vinegar
- 2 tbsp water
- 1 tbsp plus 2 tsp olive oil (divided use)
- 1/4 tsp crushed red pepper flakes
- 1 clove garlic (minced)
- 2 cup broccoli florets
- 1 lbs pork loin boneless chops (divided into 4 portions)
- 2 tbsp cilantro (chopped)

Directions:
1. In a medium bowl, combine the soy sauce, vinegar, water, 1 tablespoon olive oil, crushed red pepper, and garlic. Add the pork chops and marinate them in refrigerator for 20 minutes or longer.
2. Steam the broccoli for 5 minutes; until tender.
3. Add the remaining 2 tsp olive oil to a large sauté pan over medium-high heat. Add the pork chops and sear for about 5 minutes per side or until done. (Reserve marinade for later).
4. Place the marinade in a small saucepan. Bring it to a boil; reduce the heat and simmer about 2 minutes. Place the pork chops on serving platter and pour the cooked marinade over them.
5. Top the pork chops with chopped cilantro and serve with the steamed broccoli.

Nutrition facts:

Calories Per Serving 230; Total Fat: 13g; Sodium: 390mg; Total Carbs: 5g; Fiber: 2g; Sugars: 1g; Protein: 23g

Air-fryer Meatloaf

Servings: 6

Ingredients:
- 1 pound 90%-lean ground beef
- ½ pound ground pork
- 1 large egg, lightly beaten
- ½ cup Italian-seasoned panko breadcrumbs
- ¼ cup finely chopped yellow onion
- ¼ cup chopped fresh parsley
- 1 ½ tablespoons Worcestershire sauce
- 2 cloves garlic, minced
- ½ teaspoon kosher salt
- ½ teaspoon ground pepper
- 5 tablespoons ketchup, divided

Directions:
1. Preheat air fryer to 350°F for 5 minutes. Combine ground beef, ground pork, egg, panko, onion, parsley, Worcestershire, garlic, salt, pepper and 3 tablespoons ketchup in a large bowl; mix until well combined. Divide the mixture in half and form each half into a loaf (3-by-6-by-1 1/2 inches).
2. Place the meatloaves in the air-fryer basket. Cook until an instant-read thermometer inserted in the center registers 155°F, about 25 minutes. Brush the meatloaves with the remaining 2 tablespoons ketchup. Continue cooking until an instant-read thermometer registers 165°F, about 3 minutes. Let the meatloaves rest for 5 minutes before slicing.

Nutrition facts:
Calories Per Serving 255; Total Fat: 13g; Sodium: 476mg; Total Carbs: 11g; Fiber:1 g; Sugars: 3g; Protein: 24g

Air-fryer Empanadas

Servings: 12

Ingredients:
- 1 teaspoon extra-virgin olive oil
- ½ cup chopped yellow onion
- ½ cup chopped red or yellow bell pepper
- 8 ounces 90%-lean ground beef
- 1 tablespoon salt-free taco seasoning mix
- ½ teaspoon salt
- ¼ teaspoon ground pepper
- 1 large egg
- 1 tablespoon water
- All-purpose flour for rolling
- 3 refrigerated pie crusts (1 1/2 packages)
- Chimichurri Sauce for serving

Directions:
1. Heat oil in a large skillet over medium heat. Add onion and bell pepper and cook until translucent, about 5 minutes. Add beef and cook, stirring with a wooden spoon to crumble, until browned, about 5 minutes. Add taco seasoning, salt and pepper; cook, stirring, for 1 minute. Remove from heat and let cool for 10 minutes.
2. Preheat air fryer to 400°F for 5 minutes. Whisk egg and water in small bowl; set aside.
3. On a lightly floured surface, roll pie crusts into 11-inch circles. Using a biscuit cutter, cut 4 (4 1/2-inch) rounds from each pie crust.
4. Place 2 tablespoons beef filling in the center of each round. Brush egg wash around the edge of each crust and fold the dough in half, covering the filling. Crimp or pleat the edges to seal.
5. Coat the air-fryer basket with cooking spray. Place 6 empanadas in the basket. Brush the empanadas with egg wash and cook until golden brown, 8 to 12

minutes. Repeat with the remaining empanadas. Serve with chimichurri sauce, if desired.

Nutrition facts:

Calories Per Serving 200; Total Fat:12 g; Sodium: 312mg; Total Carbs: 20g; Sugars: 1g; Protein: 6g

Beef Stroganoff

Servings:5

Ingredients:

- 5 oz Ronzoni Healthy Harvest Whole Grain egg noodles (uncooked)
- 2 tsp olive oil
- 1 lbs beef tenderloin (sliced into 2-inch strips)
- 1 1/2 cup white (button) mushrooms (sliced)
- 1/2 cup onion(s) (minced)
- 1 tbsp all-purpose flour
- 1/2 cup dry white wine
- 1 tsp Dijon Mustard
- 1 (14.5-oz) can fat free, low sodium beef broth
- 1/2 cup fat-free sour cream
- 1/4 tsp salt (optional)
- 1/4 tsp black pepper

Directions:

1. Cook noodles according to package directions, omitting salt.
2. Add oil to a large sauté pan over high heat. Add meat and sauté for about 3 minutes. Remove meat from pan. Add mushrooms and onion and sauté for 5 minutes or until beginning to brown.
3. Add flour and cook for 1 minute. Add wine to deglaze pan; cook for 2 minutes. Add Dijon mustard and beef broth; bring to a boil. Reduce heat and simmer for 5 minutes.
4. Add beef and any juices back to broth and simmer for 3 more minutes. Add sour cream, salt (optional), and pepper; simmer for 30 seconds.
5. Serve over whole-grain egg noodles.

Nutrition facts:

Calories Per Serving 275; Total Fat:7g; Sodium: 250mg; Total Carbs: 29g; Fiber: 4g; Sugars: 3g; Protein: 23g

Jamaican Pork Tenderloin Roast

Servings:4

Cooking Time: 20 Minutes

Ingredients:

- 1 lbs lean pork tenderloin (well trimmed)
- 1/2 cup plus 3 tbsp apricot or mango nectar (not from concentrate) (divided)
- 2 green onion (scallion) (green and white parts, thinly sliced, divided)
- 3 tbsp lower sodium soy sauce
- 1 1/2 tsp grapeseed or safflower oil
- 1 tbsp fresh gingerroot (grated)
- 1/4 tsp ground cinnamon
- 1/4 tsp hot pepper sauce

Directions:

1. Place the pork in a large sealable food container. In a medium bowl, whisk together 1/2 cup of the nectar, half of the scallions, the soy sauce, oil, gingerroot, cinnamon, and hot pepper sauce. Pour the mixture into the container, seal tightly, and refrigerate at least 4 hours or overnight, rotating the pork occasionally. Separately cover and chill the remaining nectar and scallions.

2. Preheat the oven to 450°F. Remove the nectar and scallion from the refrigerator. Place the marinated pork on an unbleached parchment paper–lined baking pan. Discard the remaining marinade. (Alternatively, you can boil the remaining marinade for at least 2 minutes for safe use as a sauce with the meal.) Roast the pork until cooked through, but very slightly pink in the middle, about 20 minutes (or to an internal temperature of 145°F). Let stand at least 5 minutes before slicing.
3. Cut the pork into 24 slices. Fan out 6 slices per plate. Drizzle with reserved nectar, garnish with remaining scallion, and serve.

Nutrition facts:
Calories Per Serving 170; Total Fat: 4.5g; Sodium: 490mg; Total Carbs: 7g; Fiber: 1g; Sugars: 2g; Protein: 22g

Air Fryer Instant Pot Vortex Pork Tenderloin

Servings:4
Cooking Time: 28 Minutes

Ingredients:
- 1 lb pork tenderloin
- Cooking oil spray of choice
- 1 tbsp grain mustard
- 1 tbsp dijon mustard
- 2 tbsp honey (or substitute Vita Fiber for Keto option)
- 2 tbsp soy sauce
- 1 tbsp minced garlic
- 1 tsp sriracha sauce (adjust to taste)

Directions:

1. Mix the soy sauce, mustard, honey (or Vita Fiber), garlic, and sriracha and pour into a large baggie
2. Add the pork tenderloin and marinate from a few minutes to up to 24 hours
3. Preheat the air fryer to 380 degrees
4. Spray the air fryer tray with cooking oil and place the tenderloin on the tray and brush with extra sauce.
5. Air fry for approximately 26 minutes, turning the tenderloin every 4-5 minutes and brushing with sauce each time. The roast will get very dark brown.
6. The pork is done when a thermometer inserted lengthwise into the thickest part of the meat registers at lest 145 degree. Cook to 165 for well done.
7. Let the pork rest covered in foil for 5-10 minutes
8. Slice, serve and enjoy!

Nutrition facts:
Calories Per Serving: 324; Total Fat: 11g; Sodium: 910mg; Total Carbs: 14g; Fiber: 1g; Sugars: 12g; Protein: 41g

Air-fryer Meatballs

Servings:8

Ingredients:
- Cooking spray
- 1 pound 90%-lean ground beef
- 1 small yellow onion, grated (about 1/2 cup)
- ¼ cup grated Parmesan cheese
- 3 tablespoons whole-wheat panko breadcrumbs
- 1 large egg, lightly beaten
- 1 teaspoon Italian seasoning
- ¾ teaspoon salt
- ½ teaspoon garlic powder
- ¼ teaspoon onion powder

- ¼ teaspoon ground pepper
- Marinara sauce for serving

Directions:

1. Preheat air fryer to 370°F for 10 minutes. Lightly coat the air-fryer basket with cooking spray.
2. Mix beef, onion, Parmesan, panko, egg, Italian seasoning, salt, garlic powder, onion powder and pepper in a medium bowl just until combined. Form the beef mixture into 16 (1 1/2-inch) meatballs.
3. Working in batches if necessary, arrange the meatballs in the fryer basket in a single layer. Coat the tops of the meatballs with cooking spray. Cook until lightly browned on top and an instant-read thermometer inserted in the center registers 165°F, about 8 minutes. Serve with marinara sauce, if desired.

Nutrition facts:

Calories Per Serving 119; Total Fat: 6g; Sodium: 307mg; Total Carbs:3 g; Sugars: 1g; Protein: 13g

Air-fryer Lemony Lamb Chops With Fennel & Olives

Servings:2

Ingredients:

- 4 teaspoons lemon zest, divided, plus lemon wedges for serving
- ½ teaspoon salt
- ¼ teaspoon ground pepper
- 4 lamb loin chops
- 8 ounces baby yellow potatoes, scrubbed and halved
- 1 fennel bulb, trimmed (2-3 tablespoons fronds reserved and chopped), quartered, cored and sliced
- 1 tablespoon extra-virgin olive oil
- ¼ cup Kalamata olives, chopped

Directions:

1. Lightly coat the basket of a 6- to 9-quart air fryer with cooking spray. Preheat to 380°F for 5 minutes.
2. Combine 2 teaspoons lemon zest, salt and pepper in a large bowl. Rub half the mixture over lamb chops. Add potatoes, sliced fennel and oil to the remaining lemon zest mixture in the bowl; toss to coat.
3. Working in batches as necessary, arrange the chops and vegetables in a single layer in the prepared basket.
4. Cook, flipping once, until an instant-read thermometer inserted in the center of a chop registers 145°F, 10 to 12 minutes.
5. Meanwhile, toss olives, the reserved fennel fronds and the remaining 2 teaspoons lemon zest in a bowl. Top the chops and vegetables with the olive mixture. Serve with lemon wedges, if desired.

Nutrition facts:

Calories Per Serving350; Total Fat: 14g; Sodium: 906mg; Total Carbs: 34g; Fiber: 9g; Sugars: 8g; Protein:28 g

Signature Skillet Supper

Servings:6

Cooking Time: 30 Minutes

Ingredients:

- 1 tsp Extra Virgin Olive Oil
- 1 lbs lean ground beef (I used 93% lean)
- 1 cup onion(s) (chopped)
- 2 clove garlic (minced)

- 4 cup frozen mixed vegetables
- 2 tsp togarashi (Japanese pepper blend)
- 3 cup uncooked no yolk medium noodles
- 4 cup beef broth (low-sodium)
- 1 cup water

Directions:

1. Place olive oil in large sauté pan or skillet. Add beef, onions, and garlic and cook until beef is browned. Add vegetables and the seasoning, and mix well. Add the noodles and mix well. Add the broth and enough water to cover everything.
2. Bring to a boil. Reduce heat to medium and cook until noodles are tender, approximately 15 minutes.

Nutrition facts:

Calories Per Serving 285; Total Fat: 8g; Sodium:165mg; Total Carbs: 28g; Fiber: 6g; Sugars: 5g; Protein: 23g

Classic Meatloaf

Servings:6
Cooking Time: 55 Minutes

Ingredients:

- 2 tsp olive oil
- 1 small onion (minced)
- 1/3 cup green or red bell pepper (finely minced)
- 4 oz white (button) mushrooms (chopped)
- 2 clove garlic (minced)
- 1 tsp Italian seasoning
- 1/4 tsp sea salt
- 1/4 tsp freshly ground black pepper
- 1 lbs ground beef (95% lean)
- 1 eggs (beaten)
- 1 cup whole-wheat panko breadcrumbs
- 1 cup milk (fat-free)
- 2 tsp Worcestershire sauce
- 1/2 tsp liquid smoke (optional)
- 1/3 cup ketchup (sugar-free, such as Walden Farms)
- 1 1/2 tbsp Dijon Mustard
- 1 tsp brown sugar

Directions:

1. Preheat the oven to 375°F. Line a baking sheet with parchment paper. Set aside.
2. Heat the oil in a medium skillet over medium heat. Sauté the onion for 3 minutes. Add in the green pepper and mushrooms and sauté for 3 minutes. Add in the garlic, Italian seasoning, salt, and pepper and sauté for 1 minute.
3. Add the onion mixture to a bowl, and let cool for 2 minutes. Add in the beef, egg, breadcrumbs, milk, Worcestershire sauce, and liquid smoke, if using. Mix gently, do not over handle the meat.
4. Place the mixture onto the prepared baking sheet and form into an oblong loaf. Combine the ketchup, mustard, and brown sugar and pour over the meatloaf.
5. Bake the meatloaf for 40-45 minutes until cooked through. Remove from the oven and let the meatloaf rest 5-7 minutes prior to slicing.

Nutrition facts:

Calories Per Serving 210; Total Fat: 7g; Sodium:440 mg; Total Carbs:17 g; Fiber: 2g; Sugars: 5g; Protein: 21g

Keto Pork Chops - Super Crispy!

Servings: 4

Cooking Time: 20 Minutes

Ingredients:
- 4 1-2 inch thick boneless pork chops
- 1 3 ounce Bag pork rinds, crushed in the food processor
- 1 teaspoon Kosher Salt
- 1 teaspoon Smoked paprika
- ½ teaspoon Garlic powder
- ½ teaspoon Onion powder
- 2 large Eggs, beaten

Directions:
1. In a shallow bowl, mix the crushed pork rinds with the seasonings. In a separate shallow bowl, add in the beaten eggs. One at a time, coat the pork chops in the egg, then in the pork rind mixture. Place the breaded pork chops in the air fryer.
2. For 1 inch pork chops, set the air fryer at 400F for 12 minutes and flip half way through. For 2 inch thick pork chops, set the air fryer for 20 minutes and cook half way through. Pork chops are done when an internal temperature thermometer reads 145-160F.
3. Oven Instructions
4. Place the breaded pork chops on a sheet tray and bake in a 425F oven for 15 minutes on each side or until an internal meat thermometer reads 145F.

Nutrition facts:
Calories Per Serving: 301; Total Fat: 12g; Sodium: 1027mg; Total Carbs: 0g; Fiber: 3g; Sugars: 0.4g; Protein: 43g

Air Fryer Salt And Pepper Crispy Pork Belly Crack

Servings: 4

Ingredients:
- 1 lb raw sliced pork belly strips
- 1 teaspoon sea salt
- 1/2 teaspoon pepper

Directions:
1. Cut pork belly slices into bite sized pieces with scissors
2. Toss pieces in a bowl with salt and pepper
3. Preheat air fryer for 3 minutes
4. Place pieces into air fryer at 390 for 15 minutes, checking and turning at 5 minute intervals so they get crispy all over
5. Depending on thickness of slices, they should be fully cooked in 15 minutes
6. Drain on paper towels
7. Crunch away and don't forget to share them!

Nutrition facts:
Calories Per Serving: 332; Total Fat: 24g; Sodium: 635mg; Total Carbs: 0g; Fiber: 0g; Sugars: 0g; Protein: 26g

Air Fryer Pork Chops

Servings: 4

Cooking Time: 12 Minutes

Ingredients:
- 8 oz pork chops (four) bone-in center-cut or boneless
- 1 tsp olive oil
- Pork Chop Seasoning
- 1 tsp paprika

- 1 tsp onion powder
- 1 tsp salt
- 1 tsp pepper

Directions:
1. Preheat your air fryer to 380°F.
2. Brush both sides of pork chop with a little olive oil.
3. Mix the pork seasonings together in a bowl (this is enough for four pork chops) and apply to both sides of the pork chop.
4. Place pork chop in air fryer and cook for between 9-12 minutes, turning the chop over halfway, until it reaches a minimum temp of 145°F (exact cook time will vary depending on thickness of pork and your model of air fryer)

Nutrition facts:
Calories Per Serving: 366; Total Fat: 17g; Sodium: 691mg; Total Carbs: 1g; Fiber: 1g; Sugars: 1g; Protein: 49g

Chili-cheese Nachos

Servings: 8

Ingredients:
- 1 pound lean ground beef
- ¾ cup finely chopped white onion
- ½ cup finely chopped red bell pepper
- 4 cloves garlic, chopped
- 2 tablespoons chili powder
- 1 tablespoon ground cumin
- 2 teaspoons dried oregano
- 1 teaspoon ground coriander
- 1 (14 ounce) can diced tomatoes
- ¼ cup water
- 8 ounces tortilla chips
- 2 cups shredded cheese, such as Cheddar or pepper Jack

Directions:
1. Preheat oven to 350 degrees F.
2. Cook beef, onion, bell pepper and garlic in a large skillet over medium-high heat, crumbling the beef with a spatula, until the meat is browned, 8 to 10 minutes. Stir in chili powder, cumin, oregano and coriander; cook, stirring, for 30 seconds. Add tomatoes (with their juice) and water and simmer for 5 minutes.
3. Top chips with the chili and cheese. Bake until the cheese is melted, about 7 minutes.

Nutrition facts:
Calories Per Serving384; Total Fat:22 g; Sodium: 425mg; Total Carbs: 25g; Fiber: 4g; Sugars: 3g; Protein: 21g

Pork Schnitzel With Creamy Dill Sauce

Servings:4

Ingredients:
- ¼ cup sour cream
- 2 tablespoons dill pickle relish
- 2 tablespoons chopped fresh dill, plus more for garnish
- 4 boneless pork loin chops (about 1 pound), trimmed
- 1 teaspoon garlic powder
- ¼ teaspoon salt
- 2 tablespoons all-purpose flour
- 1 large egg
- 1 cup panko breadcrumbs
- ¼ cup extra-virgin olive oil
- ⅛ teaspoon ground pepper
- 4 lemon wedges

Directions:

1. Combine sour cream, relish and dill in a small bowl. Set aside.
2. Using a meat mallet or a small heavy saucepan, pound each pork chop between pieces of plastic wrap to an even 1/4-inch thickness. Sprinkle the pork with garlic powder and salt.
3. Place flour in a shallow dish. Lightly beat egg in another shallow dish. Add panko to a third shallow dish. Dredge the pork in the flour, shaking off any excess. Dip in the egg, then dredge in the panko, pressing to adhere.
4. Heat oil in a large skillet over medium heat. Working in batches if necessary, cook the pork, flipping once, until golden and crispy and an instant-read thermometer inserted in the thickest part registers 145°F, 4 to 6 minutes. (Alternatively, use an air fryer: Coat the basket with cooking spray. Place the pork in a single layer in the basket. Cook, in batches if necessary, at 360°F until an instant-read thermometer inserted in the center registers 145°, about 10 minutes. If preparing in batches, cooking time for the second batch may be shorter.)
5. Sprinkle the pork with pepper. Garnish with additional chopped dill, if desired, and serve with the reserved sauce and lemon wedges.

Nutrition facts:

Calories Per Serving363; Total Fat: 23g; Sodium: 387mg; Total Carbs: 15g; Fiber: 1g; Sugars: 1g; Protein: 23g

POULTRY RECIPES

Chicken And Cabbage

Servings: 4

Cooking Time: 12 Minutes

Ingredients:
- 4 cups (560g) chicken diced and cooked
- 1 tablespoon olive oil
- 2 ½ tablespoons butter
- 1 tablespoon garlic paste
- ½ teaspoon smoked paprika
- 1 head green cabbage cored and chopped
- salt and pepper and other seasonings, to taste
- chopped fresh basil, to garnish

Directions:
1. Heat olive oil and butter In a skillet, over medium heat, then saute the garlic paste until bubbly.
2. Mix in paprika followed by the cabbage.
3. Sauté for 7-10 minutes until the cabbage is cooked to your taste.
4. A couple of minutes before the end of the cooking time, add the chicken and cook until it is warmed through.
5. Season with salt and pepper (and any other seasonings, if desired).
6. Garnish with chopped basil, serve, and enjoy.

Nutrition facts:
Calories Per Serving 328; Total Fat: 15g; Sodium: 278mg; Total Carbs: 15g; Fiber: 6g; Sugars: 7g; Protein: 35g

Baja Turkey Burgers

Servings: 4

Cooking Time: 10 Minutes

Ingredients:
- 12 oz lean ground turkey
- 1/2 cup salsa verde (divided use)
- 4 sprouted whole wheat buns or whole wheat english muffins
- 1 avocado (peeled and thinly sliced)
- 1/8 tsp salt
- 2 cup packaged coleslaw mix

Directions:
1. Preheat a grill to medium high.
2. In a large bowl, gently mix the turkey and ¼ cup of the salsa until just combined. Form the mixture by hand into four patties, about 4 inches in diameter.
3. Grill the burgers until well done (an internal temperature of at least 165° F), about 5 minutes per side. If desired, lightly grill the buns, too.
4. Onto the bottom portion of each bun, arrange ¼ of the avocado slices and sprinkle with the salt. Top each with a turkey burger patty, ½ cup of the coleslaw mix, and 1 Tbsp of the remaining salsa. If desired, add a slice of tomato and a lettuce leaf to each. Cover the burgers with a bun top and serve.

Nutrition facts:
Calories Per Serving 370; Total Fat: 13g; Sodium: 420mg; Total Carbs: 37g; Fiber: 10g; Sugars: 2g; Protein: 25g

Bacon Wrapped Chicken Tenders

Servings: 4

Cooking Time: 20 Minutes

Ingredients:
- 1 lb chicken tenderloins
- 1 package Applegate turkey bacon or other nitrate free turkey bacon for keto, use a no sugar pork bacon
- Sliced pepper jack sharp cheddar, or cheese of your choice
- 1 avocado
- Olive oil spray
- Garlic powder
- Himalayan salt optional

Directions:
1. Sprinkle chicken with some garlic powder and salt (if desired, I usually leave it out), then wrap each tenderloin with 1-2 pieces of bacon. The smaller tenderloins work well with one, but if your tenderloins are bigger, you might need a second one or another half. The bacon should stay wrapped easily, but if you need to, use a toothpick to keep the bacon secure.
2. Place chicken in your air fryer basket and spray with olive oil spray. Cook at 370 for ten minutes, then carefully flip and cook at 390 for 8-10 more minutes or until bacon is crisp and chicken is cooked through. Turn off air fryer.
3. Place a half slice of cheese on top of your bacon wrapped chicken and leave in the air fryer basket (air fryer turned off) until it melts.
4. Top with 1-2 T of sliced or diced avocado and enjoy!

Nutrition facts:

Calories Per Serving 588; Total Fat: 38g; Sodium: 2397mg; Total Carbs: 7g; Fiber: 3g; Sugars: 0.3g; Protein: 54g

Curry Seasoned Chicken Drumsticks

Servings: 6

Cooking Time: 40 Minutes

Ingredients:
- 2 tsp curry powder
- ¼ tsp cumin
- ¼ tsp garlic powder
- ¼ tsp salt
- ¼ tsp pepper
- 6 chicken drumsticks
- 3 tbsp plain Greek yogurt
- ½ lemon, juiced

Directions:
1. If using the oven, preheat oven to 425 degrees F. If using the air fryer, no preheating is necessary.
2. Combine the curry powder, cumin, garlic powder, salt, and pepper in a small bowl. Stir until combined.
3. Place the chicken drumsticks, Greek yogurt, lemon juice, and spice mixture in a zip top bag. Close the bag and shake it a bit, using your hands to move the chicken around so that everything is well coated. Marinate in the fridge for 30 minutes.
4. If baking in the oven: Remove the drumsticks from the bag and place them on a baking sheet, discarding any extra marinade left in the bag. Bake at 425 degrees F for 40-45 minutes, or until chicken hits an internal temperature of 165 degrees F.
5. If using the air fryer: Remove the drumsticks from the bag and place them in the basket of the air fryer,

discarding any extra marinade left in the bag. Air fry at 400 degrees F for 10 minutes. Flip, then air fry again for another 12-15 minutes, or until the chicken hits an internal temperature of 165 degrees F.

Nutrition facts:

Calories Per Serving 123; Total Fat: 2.8g; Sodium: 166mg; Total Carbs: 3.7g; Fiber: 0.3g; Sugars: 3.2g; Protein: 20.3g

Air-fryer Turkey Stuffed Peppers

Servings: 3

Ingredients:

- 3 medium red bell peppers
- 1 tablespoon olive oil
- 12 ounces ground turkey
- ½ cup cooked brown rice
- ¼ cup panko breadcrumbs
- ¾ cup low-sodium marinara sauce
- 3 tablespoons finely chopped flat-leaf parsley
- ¼ teaspoon ground pepper
- ¼ cup grated Parmesan cheese (1 oz.)
- ¼ cup shredded part-skim mozzarella cheese (1 oz.)

Directions:

1. Coat the basket of an air fryer with cooking spray. Cut tops off peppers and reserve. Seed the peppers and set aside.
2. Heat oil in a large skillet over medium-high heat. Add turkey; cook, stirring occasionally, until browned, about 4 minutes. Stir in rice and panko; cook, stirring occasionally, until warmed through, about 1 minute. Remove from heat and stir in marinara, parsley, pepper and Parmesan. Divide the mixture evenly among the prepared peppers.
3. Place the peppers in the prepared air-fryer basket. Nestle the pepper tops in the bottom of the basket. Cook at 350°F until the peppers are tender, about 8 minutes. Top with mozzarella; cook until the cheese is melted, about 2 minutes more.

Nutrition facts:

Calories Per Serving 407; Total Fat: 21g; Sodium: 340mg; Total Carbs: 26g; Fiber: 4g; Sugars: 7g; Protein: 29g

Best Air Fryer Chicken Fajitas Recipe

Servings: 4

Cooking Time: 15 Minutes

Ingredients:

- 1 lb. Boneless, skinless chicken breast
- 1 Tablespoon olive oil
- 1 Tablespoon fajita seasoning
- 2 bell peppers (any color) seeded and thinly sliced
- 1 large onion, thinly sliced
- 1 jalapeno pepper, seeded and thinly sliced (optional)
- ¼ cup chopped fresh cilantro
- 1 Tablespoon lime juice
- 8 (6 inches) tortillas (your favorite) warmed
- Desired toppings

Directions:

1. Cut the chicken into thin strips and add olive oil, fajita seasoning, bell pepper, and onion to a large, zip-top plastic bag or a large bowl. Seal the bag and turn to coat. Chill at least for 30 minutes or up to 8 hours.
2. Preheat the air fryer to 390 F for 5 minutes.
3. Spread chicken mixture in the air fryer basket, air fry for 15 minutes or until chicken is cooked

through and vegetables are tender. Shake the basket halfway through.

4. Toss together the cooked chicken, jalapeno, cilantro, and lime juice in a medium bowl. Serve with tortillas of your choice and desired toppings. Enjoy!

Nutrition facts:

Calories Per Serving 240; Total Fat: 8g; Sodium: 240mg; Total Carbs:5g; Fiber: 1g; Sugars: 2g; Protein: 36g

Turkey Skillet Casserole

Servings:2

Cooking Time: 10 Minutes

Ingredients:

- 2 tsp canola oil
- 3/4 lbs boneless turkey breast (cut into 1-inch pieces)
- 3/4 cup frozen chopped onion
- 2 tsp garlic (minced)
- 1/8 tsp salt
- 1/4 tsp freshly ground black pepper
- 3/4 cup pasta sauce (reduced-sodium, no-sugar-added)
- 1/2 cup water
- 2 cup sliced baby bella mushrooms
- 3 oz fresh whole-wheat linguine (broken into 4-5 inch pieces)
- 2 cup ready-to-eat spinach (washed)
- 1/2 cup fresh basil (torn into bite-size pieces)
- 1/4 cup sharp cheddar cheese (shredded, reduced-fat)
- 3 tbsp sour cream (reduced-fat)

Directions:

1. Heat oil in a medium=size nonstick skillet over medium-high heat. Add turkey, onion and garlic. Sauté 3 minutes, turning turkey pieces to brown all sides. Sprinkle with salt and pepper.
2. Add the pasta sauce, water, mushrooms and linguine. Stir to mix well. Bring to a simmer. Reduce heat to medium, cover with a lid, and cook 3 minutes. The linguine should be cooked through. Add a little water if sauce is dry before pasta is cooked.
3. Add spinach and basil, stirring until spinach wilts. Remove from the heat and sprinkle the cheese on top. Spoon sour cream over cheese. Serve on 2 dinner plates.

Nutrition facts:

Calories Per Serving 540; Total Fat: 13g; Sodium: 550mg; Total Carbs: 51g; Fiber: 8g; Sugars:11g; Protein: 56g

Sweet Chili Chicken, Sweet Potatoes, And Broccoli

Servings:4

Ingredients:

- 2 med sweet potatoes (peeled and medium diced)
- 2 Tbsp + 1 tsp olive oil (divided)
- 1/4 tsp salt
- 2 breasts, approx. 8 oz. boneless, skinless chicken breasts (sliced into 4 thin filets)
- 1 large crown broccoli (divided into florets (approx. 1 lb.))
- 2 tbsp Sweet Chili sauce

Directions:

1. Preheat the oven to 425 degrees F. Line a large baking sheet with parchment paper.
2. Toss the sweet potatoes with 1 tablespoon of olive oil and salt. Add to the baking sheet in a single layer. Place in the oven and bake for 10 minutes.

3. Meanwhile, preheat a large skillet over medium-high heat.
4. Once the skillet is hot, add 1 tablespoon of oil and chicken. Sear until golden brown on both sides (but not cooked through). Remove from heat.
5. Once the sweet potatoes have been baking for 10 minutes, remove the baking sheet and add the chicken and broccoli. Drizzle the broccoli with the remaining 1 teaspoon of olive oil.
6. Place the baking sheet in the oven and continue to cook until the chicken is cooked through and the veggies tender.
7. Remove from oven and divide between plates. Drizzle with sweet chili sauce and serve.

Nutrition facts:
Calories Per Serving 290; Total Fat: 11g; Sodium: 350mg; Total Carbs: 20g; Fiber:4g; Sugars: 8g; Protein: 27g

Easy Keto Pizza Chicken Bake

Servings:12
Cooking Time: 25 Minutes

Ingredients:
- 2 lbs. chicken breasts (approx 4 chicken breasts cut into bite-sized cubes)
- 3 TB butter
- 1 TB olive oil
- 1/2 tsp basil
- 2 tsp garlic powder
- 1 tsp onion powder
- 1/4 tsp Italian seasoning
- 1/2 tsp salt
- 1/2 tsp pepper
- 1/4 tsp crushed red pepper
- 20 oz low carb spaghetti sauce (about ¾ of a 24 oz jar)
- 2 ½ cups mozzarella cheese
- 1/4 cup Parmesan cheese
- 20-24 small pepperoni
- ¼ large green pepper
- ¼ medium onion
- 2 TB mushrooms sliced
- 1 tsp parsley

Directions:
1. Preheat oven to 400° F.
2. Grease a 9 X 13 casserole dish.
3. Cut chicken into bite-sized pieces and place them in a bowl. Add the spices and mix well to coat the chicken.
4. Add 3 TB butter and 1 TB olive oil a large skillet over medium-high heat. (I used a 12-inch skillet.)
5. Once the skillet is hot, add the chicken in a single layer and brown both sides nicely. (The chicken will turn easily once it has fully browned.)
6. Using a slotted spoon, scoop out the chicken spreading it evenly onto the bottom of your greased casserole dish.
7. Top with 20 oz spaghetti sauce (approx ¾ of a 24 oz jar) and spread it out evenly.
8. Top with 2 ½ cups of mozzarella cheese and ¼ cup Parmesan cheese.
9. Add pepperoni, green peppers, mushrooms, and onions to the top.
10. Bake for 15 minutes then move to the top shelf of the oven and broil for 2 minutes or until the mozzarella cheese begins to bubble and turn brown.
11. Let sit for 5 - 10 minutes before serving. The spaghetti sauce will be a bit thin when you first take it out of the oven but will thicken up if you let it sit for a few minutes.

Nutrition facts:

Calories Per Serving 248; Total Fat: 16g; Sodium: 481mg; Total Carbs: 3g; Fiber: 1g; Sugars: 1g; Protein: 23g

Chicken Satay

Servings:4
Cooking Time: 10 Minutes

Ingredients:
- 8 bamboo skewers
- 1 lbs boneless, skinless chicken breasts
- 2 tbsp Splenda Brown Sugar blend (divided use)
- 2 tbsp lower sodium soy sauce (divided use)
- 2 clove garlic (minced, divided use)
- 1 tsp minced fresh ginger
- 2 tbsp lime juice
- 1/2 tsp Asian-style hot sauce, such as sriracha
- 2 tbsp creamy peanut butter
- 1/4 cup unsweetened coconut milk beverage

Directions:
1. Soak bamboo skewers in warm water for at least 30 minutes. While skewers are soaking, slice chicken breasts into eight strips lengthwise.
2. In a medium bowl, whisk together 1 tbsp Splenda Brown Sugar, 1 tbsp soy sauce, half the minced garlic, ginger, lime juice and hot sauce. Add chicken to the marinade and marinate chicken strips in the refrigerator for 1 hour.
3. Prepare an indoor or outdoor grill.
4. While the chicken is marinating, whisk together the remaining tbsp Splenda brown sugar blend, remaining tbsp soy sauce, remaining minced garlic, peanut butter, and coconut milk in a microwave safe bowl. Set aside.
5. Thread chicken strips lengthwise onto the soaked bamboo skewers. Grill chicken for 4-5 minutes one each side.
6. Right before serving, microwave sauce for 30 seconds. Remove from microwave and whisk again to combine. Serve two skewers with 2 Tbsps. of sauce.

Nutrition facts:
Calories Per Serving 220; Total Fat: 7g; Sodium: 380mg; Total Carbs: 10g; Fiber: 1g; Sugars: 4g; Protein:2 7g

Asian Chicken Salad

Servings:4

Ingredients:
- 9 oz romaine lettuce (chopped)
- 1 cup cabbage (shredded)
- 1 cup shredded carrots
- 1/4 cup slivered almonds (toasted)
- 1 tbsp plus 1 tsp Toasted sesame seeds (divided use)
- 2 cup cooked chicken breast (diced)
- 2 tbsp rice vinegar
- 2 tbsp lower sodium soy sauce
- 2 tbsp olive oil
- 1/4 tsp crushed red pepper flakes

Directions:
1. In a medium bowl mix together cabbage, lettuce, almonds, 1 tablespoon sesame seeds, and chicken.
2. In a small bowl whisk together vinegar, soy sauce, and oil.
3. Pour dressing over salad and toss to coat. Top with remaining 1 teaspoon sesame seeds and red pepper flakes.

Nutrition facts:
Calories Per Serving 270; Total Fat: 15g; Sodium: 470mg; Total Carbs: 9g; Fiber: 4g; Sugars: 3g; Protein: 26g

Instant Pot Chicken Sausage And Zucchini Stuffed Potatoes

Servings:4

Cooking Time: 30 Minutes

Ingredients:

- 2 tbsp extra virgin olive oil (divided use)
- 2 links (6 oz total) fully cooked Italian-style chicken sausage links, such as Al Fresco (chopped)
- 2 cup water (divided use)
- 1 zucchini (chopped)
- 1 cup green onion (scallion) (chopped, divided use)
- 1/2 tsp dried oregano
- 1 tsp hot sauce, such as Frank's
- 4 (8-oz each) russet or baking potatoes (pierced in several areas with a fork)
- 1/8 tsp salt
- 1/4 tsp black pepper
- 1 oz reduced-fat blue cheese (crumbled)

Directions:

1. Press the Saute/Browning button. When hot, add 1 Tbsp. oil, tilt the pressure cooker pot to coat bottom lightly. Add sausage and cook 3 minutes or until beginning to brown on edges. Add 1/3 cup of the water, the zucchini, 3/4 cup of the onion and oregano, cook 3 minutes or until zucchini is tender crisp, scraping up browned bits. Place in a medium bowl with hot sauce and remaining 1 Tbsp. oil. Cover to keep warm.
2. Put a steamer basket in the pressure cooking pot and add the remaining water. Top with the potatoes. Lock the lid in place and close the seal valve. Press the Cancel button and reset to Manual for 18 minutes. When time ends, use a 10-minute natural pressure release, then a quick pressure release.
3. When valve drops, carefully remove the lid. Remove potatoes with tongs (or a fork). Split potatoes almost in half and fluff with a fork. Add the salt and pepper to the sausage mixture and spoon equal amounts over each potato. Top with the cheese and remaining 1/4 cup green onion.

Nutrition facts:

Calories Per Serving 350; Total Fat: 12g; Sodium: 470mg; Total Carbs: 45g; Fiber:6g; Sugars: 6g; Protein: 16g

Sheet Pan Chicken, Green Beans & Potatoes

Servings:4

Cooking Time: 30 Minutes

Ingredients:

- 2 medium (2 cups chopped) red potatoes (chopped into bite-sized pieces)
- 1 tsp olive oil
- 16 oz chicken tenderloins
- 10 oz frozen cut green beans
- 4 tbsp unsalted butter
- 1 tbsp Italian dressing mix

Directions:

1. Preheat oven to 400° F.
2. To "leach" the potatoes: Place chopped potatoes in a large pan and cover completely with water. Bring to a boil, then drain. Refill water over the potatoes, to cover by 1-inch. Bring to a boil again and boil for 10 minutes. Drain and toss with 1 teaspoon olive oil before adding to the sheet pan.
3. **This step is optional and helps reduce the potassium content of the potatoes for people on a potassium-restricted diet.

4. Spray a 9 x13-inch sheet pan with cooking spray. Place the raw chicken strips down 1/3 of the pan. Place the potatoes down another 1/3 of the pan. Finally, lay the frozen green beans down the last 1/3 of the pan.
5. Melt the butter and drizzle over the entire pan of chicken, potatoes and green beans. Sprinkle Italian dressing dry mix over the entire pan.
6. Bake for 20 to 30 minutes. Check chicken for doneness after 20 minutes.

Nutrition facts:
Calories Per Serving 330; Total Fat: 17g; Sodium: 310mg; Total Carbs: 19g; Fiber: 2.5g; Sugars: 1g; Protein: 25g

Air-fryer Spinach & Feta Turkey Burgers

Servings:2

Ingredients:
- 8 ounces ground turkey breast
- 1 ½ tablespoons extra-virgin olive oil
- 2 teaspoons chopped fresh oregano
- ½ teaspoon crushed red pepper
- ¼ teaspoon salt
- 2 garlic cloves, grated
- ½ cup baby spinach leaves
- ¼ cup thinly sliced red onion
- ½ tablespoon red-wine vinegar
- ¼ cup crumbled feta cheese
- 2 whole-wheat burger buns, split and toasted

Directions:
1. Lightly coat air-fryer basket with cooking spray.
2. Combine turkey, oil, oregano, crushed red pepper, salt and garlic in a bowl. Mix well. Form the mixture into 2 (1/2-inch-thick) patties. Place in the prepared air-fryer basket and cook at 360°F, turning once, until an instant-read thermometer inserted in the center registers 155°F, 13 to 15 minutes.
3. Toss spinach, onion and vinegar together. Divide feta among top and bottom halves of buns. Place the burgers on the bottom halves of the buns. Top with the spinach mixture and the bun tops.
4. Air-Fryer Zucchini Fries

Nutrition facts:
Calories Per Serving351; Total Fat: 16g; Sodium: 777mg; Total Carbs: 26g; Fiber: 4g; Sugars: 2g; Protein: 28g

Air-fryer Turkey Breast

Servings:6

Ingredients:
- 3 tablespoons extra-virgin olive oil
- 1 tablespoon chopped fresh rosemary
- ¾ teaspoon salt
- ¾ teaspoon ground pepper
- 1 (1 1/2- to 2-pound) boneless, skin-on turkey breast
- 1 tablespoon thinly sliced garlic

Directions:
1. Line bottom of air fryer basket with foil; preheat to 350°F for 5 minutes.
2. Meanwhile, stir oil, rosemary, salt and pepper together in a small bowl. Pat turkey breast dry using paper towels; gently loosen the skin by running your fingers between it and the meat. Rub the oil mixture on both sides and under the skin. Arrange garlic slices evenly under the skin.
3. Place the turkey breast, skin-side down, in the prepared basket; cook for 20 minutes. Flip skin-side up; cook until an instant-read thermometer

inserted near the center registers 165°F, 15 to 20 minutes. Transfer to a cutting board and loosely cover with foil; let rest for 10 minutes. Slice into 1/2-inch-thick slices and serve warm.

Nutrition facts:

Calories Per Serving 206; Total Fat: 12g; Sodium: 343mg; Total Carbs: 1g; Protein: 22g

Air-fryer Chicken Cordon Bleu

Servings:4

Ingredients:

- 4 boneless skinless chicken breast halves (4 ounces each)
- 1/4 teaspoon salt
- 1/4 teaspoon pepper
- 4 slices deli ham
- 2 slices aged Swiss cheese, halved
- 1 cup panko bread crumbs
- Cooking spray
- SAUCE:
- 1 tablespoon all-purpose flour
- 1/2 cup 2% milk
- 1/4 cup dry white wine
- 3 tablespoons finely shredded Swiss cheese
- 1/8 teaspoon salt
- Dash pepper

Directions:

1. Preheat air fryer to 365°. Sprinkle chicken breasts with salt and pepper. Place on greased tray in air-fryer basket. Cook 10 minutes. Top each chicken breast with 1 slice ham and 1/2 slice cheese, folding ham in half and covering chicken as much as possible. Sprinkle with bread crumbs. Carefully spritz crumbs with cooking spray. Cook until a thermometer inserted in chicken reads 165°, 5-7 minutes longer.

2. For sauce, in a small saucepan, whisk flour and milk until smooth. Bring to a boil, stirring constantly; cook and stir until thickened, 1-2 minutes.

3. Reduce to medium heat. Add wine and cheese; cook and stir 2-3 minutes or until cheese is melted and sauce is thickened and bubbly. Stir in salt and pepper. Keep warm over low heat until ready to serve. Serve with chicken.

Nutrition facts:

Calories Per Serving 262; Total Fat: 9.9g; Sodium: 762mg; Total Carbs: 25.3g; Fiber: 1.7g; Sugars: 3.4g; Protein: 14.8g

Chicken Fried Rice

Servings:4

Cooking Time: 10 Minutes

Ingredients:

- 3 Tbs sesame oil (or canola oil)
- 1 lbs skinless chicken breast, cut into ½ inch pieces
- 1 Tbs minced garlic
- ½ cup sweet onion, diced
- ¼ cup bell pepper, any color, diced
- ¼ cup carrots, diced
- ½ cup peas, frozen or fresh
- 3 eggs, beaten
- 1 package RightRice Fried Rice Medley https://rightrice.com/products/rightrice-medley-fried-rice
- 3 Tsp low sodium soy sauce
- Salt & pepper to taste

Directions:

1. In a large non-stick pan or wok, bring oil over medium heat and add chicken. Cook for 5-6 minutes, flipping intermittently, so chicken cooks evenly and reaches an internal temperature of 165 F.

Note: cook time will vary on the size and thickness of chicken pieces.
2. While the chicken is cooking, prepare RightRice Fried Rice Medley in a separate pot according to package directions.
3. Remove chicken from pan, leaving juices behind.
4. Add vegetables and garlic. Cook for 3-5 minutes, until they begin to soften, stirring occasionally.
5. Move vegetables to one side of pan and add whisked eggs to the other side. Scramble eggs until cooked throughout.
6. Add chicken and prepared RightRice into the pan. Drizzle with soy sauce and mix evenly. Add salt and pepper to taste if desired.
7. Cook for an additional 2-3 minutes until vegetables are tender and chicken is reheated. Serve warm.
8. Makes 4 servings.

Nutrition facts:

Calories Per Serving 302; Total Fat: 17g; Sodium: 312mg; Total Carbs: 7g; Fiber: 2g; Sugars: 3g; Protein: 30g

Crock Pot Moo Shu Chicken

Servings: 4
Cooking Time: 6 Hours

Ingredients:
- 12 oz broccoli slaw
- 3 carrots (shredded)
- 1 lbs boneless, skinless chicken breasts (thinly sliced)
- 3 tbsp hoisin sauce
- 1/4 cup water
- 3 clove garlic (minced)
- 1 tsp lower sodium soy sauce
- 1 tbsp Cornstarch
- 4 leaves bibb or boston lettuce

Directions:
1. Layer the slaw mix and carrots in the bottom of crockpot. Top with the chicken.
2. In a small bowl, mix the hoisin sauce, water, garlic, soy sauce, and cornstarch. Pour over the chicken mixture and set the crockpot to high for 4-6 hours.
3. Serve 1 1/2 cups of the mixture in each lettuce leaf.

Nutrition facts:

Calories Per Serving 210; Total Fat: 2.5g; Sodium: 380mg; Total Carbs: 18g; Fiber: 4g; Sugars: 8g; Protein: 29g

Air-fryer Chicken Tenders

Servings: 4

Ingredients:
- ¼ cup whole-wheat flour
- 2 large eggs, beaten
- 1 cup whole-wheat panko breadcrumbs
- 2 teaspoons Italian seasoning
- 1 pound chicken tenders
- ¼ teaspoon ground pepper
- Cooking spray
- ½ teaspoon salt
- Honey mustard for serving

Directions:
1. Preheat air fryer to 400°F for 10 minutes.
2. Place flour in a shallow bowl. Place eggs in a separate shallow bowl. Combine panko and Italian seasoning in a separate shallow bowl, stirring to combine.
3. Sprinkle chicken tenders with pepper. Working with 1 tender at a time, dredge the chicken in the flour, shaking off excess. Dip in the eggs to coat, letting excess drip off. Dredge in the panko mixture, pressing to adhere. Transfer to a large plate.

4. Working in batches if necessary, generously coat all sides of the chicken with cooking spray. Add the breaded chicken to the fryer basket; cook, flipping once, until crispy and a thermometer inserted in the thickest portion registers at least 165°F, about 8 to 10 minutes. Sprinkle with salt. Serve with honey mustard, if desired.

Nutrition facts:

Calories Per Serving 232; Total Fat: 5g; Sodium: 449mg; Total Carbs: 15g; Fiber: 2g; Sugars: 1g; Protein:32 g

Homemade Air Fryer Sweet Potato Chicken Nuggets

Servings:24

Cooking Time: 16 Minutes

Ingredients:
- 2 cups whole grain crackers I used simple mills almond flour crackers
- 1 sweet potato 1 cup
- 1 lb ground chicken 93% or 99%
- 1/2 tsp garlic powder
- 1/2 tsp onion powder
- 1/4 cup oat flour
- 1/2 tsp salt Optional

Directions:
1. Add crackers to a food processor and grind into a coarse flour. Remove from food processor and set aside in a medium-size bowl. Add sweet potato to the food processor and pulse until the sweet potato is diced.
2. Add in ground chicken, oat flour, and seasonings to the sweet potato. Turn on the food processor and let it combine in the ingredients (you do not need to pulse.) You may need to scrape down the sides and turn back on once, but I usually don't need to.
3. Using 2-3 tablespoons of chicken mixture form oval or square chicken nugget shape, coat in ground crackers. Place on a parchment-lined baking sheet. Once you have 12-16 chicken nuggets, preheat the air fryer to 360F.
4. Once your air fryer is preheated, spray the tray with avocado oil. Add the chicken nuggets, then spray the top of them with more avocado oil. Cook for 16 minutes, turning each one over at the halfway mark.
5. To freeze uncooked chicken nuggets:
6. Freeze the entire sheet pan of chicken nuggets. Once they are frozen, they can then be transferred to another storage container for the freezer. When you are ready to make them, preheat the air fryer to 360F.
7. Once your air fryer is preheated, spray the tray with avocado oil. Add the chicken nuggets, then spray the top of them with more avocado oil. Cook for 18 minutes, turning each one over at the halfway mark.
8. To freeze cooked chicken nuggets:
9. Cool in the refrigerator, then place chicken nuggets in a freezer container, like a freezer bag. You can microwave for 2 minutes to reheat or put them in the air fryer for 8-10 minutes.
10. No air fryer?
11. Spray the top of the chicken nuggets with avocado oil and bake at 400F for 20-30 minutes, turning over at the 10-minute mark.

Nutrition facts:

Calories Per Serving 85; Total Fat: 3g; Sodium: 137mg; Total Carbs: 10g; Fiber: 1g; Sugars: 2g; Protein: 4g

Greek Chicken Kabobs

Servings: 6

Cooking Time: 15 Minutes

Ingredients:
- 1 ½ pounds boneless skinless chicken breast cubed
- 8 ounces cremini mushrooms rinsed and blotted dry
- 2 zucchini halved and sliced
- 2 red bell peppers seeded and chopped into big pieces
- 1 small red onion halved and thickly sliced
- 12 to 14 wooden or metal skewers
- Easy Greek Marinade
- ¾ cup olive oil
- 1 tablespoon Greek seasoning
- 1 teaspoon dried thyme
- 1 teaspoon dried rosemary
- 2 teaspoons minced garlic
- 1 lemon juiced
- ½ teaspoon salt
- fresh ground black pepper
- Feta Dill Sauce
- ¾ cup nonfat plain Greek yogurt
- ¼ cup mayonnaise I like olive oil mayonnaise
- ¼ cup crumbled feta
- ½ lemon juiced
- ½ teaspoon minced garlic
- 1 to 2 tablespoons fresh chopped dill (plus additional for garnish) or 1 to 2 teaspoons dried dill weed
- salt and freshly ground black pepper to taste

Directions:
1. Soak wooden skewers in water for at least 30 minutes in advance of assembling kabobs.
2. For the Easy Greek Marinade
3. Combine the marinade ingredients in a small bowl and set aside.
4. Place the cubed chicken in a gallon sized resealable plastic storage bag. Pour half the marinade over the chicken, seal the bag and turn the bag several times to distribute the marinade. Repeat this process in a separate bag with the vegetables and the remaining marinade. Refrigerate the chicken and veggies for 3 to 6 hours.
5. For the Feta Dill Sauce
6. Combine ingredients for Feta Dill Sauce in a small bowl. Cover and refrigerate until ready to serve. The sauce can be made up to 8 hours in advance.
7. Assemble the Greek Chicken Kabobs
8. Line a baking sheet with foil (for easy cleanup) and set aside. Prepare and preheat the grill.
9. While the grill is heating, thread the marinated chicken and veggies onto the water-soaked skewers and transfer to the prepared baking sheet for easy transport to the grill. I usually use 3 cubes of chicken per skewer and alternate with a mixture of the vegetables. Refrigerate the assembled kabobs, if needed, until the grill is ready.
10. Grilling Instructions
11. Grill kabobs over low heat, turning occasionally until the chicken is thoroughly cooked and the vegetables are tender. The chicken should register 165 degrees F when tested with an instant read thermometer.
12. Garnish the Feta Dill Sauce with a little fresh dill, if desired, and serve with the Greek Chicken Kabobs.

Nutrition facts:

Calories Per Serving 484; Total Fat: 35g; Sodium: 486mg; Total Carbs: 13g; Fiber: 3g; Sugars: 7g; Protein: 30g

Creamy Tomato Chicken

Servings: 4

Cooking Time: 20 Minutes

Ingredients:

- 3 large (1 ½ pounds/650g) chicken breasts boneless and skinless, sliced into 6 cutlets and pounded to an even thickness
- 1/2 teaspoon Italian seasoning
- 1/2 teaspoon salt
- 1/4 teaspoon ground black pepper
- 1/4 cup all purpose flour
- 1 tablespoon butter
- 1 tablespoon olive oil
- 3 cloves garlic minced
- 3 tablespoons tomato paste
- 1 cup heavy whipping cream
- 1/4 cup grated parmesan cheese
- 1 roma tomato diced
- chopped fresh basil for garnish

Directions:

1. Season chicken cutlets with italian seasoning, salt and pepper. Dredge in flour, and shake off any excess flour.
2. In a skillet, melt butter and heat oil. When shimmering, add the chicken and cook the cutlets on both sides until cooked through. The chicken is done when the internal temperature reaches 165°F/74°C using a kitchen thermometer. This takes 4-5 minutes per side, depending on the thickness of the cutlets. Remove onto a plate and keep warm.
3. Add garlic, and cook for 30 seconds. Then add the tomato paste and the heavy cream and whisk until well combined. If the sauce is too thick, add a splash of water.
4. Add parmesan, and stir it in until melted, then add the tomato and let the sauce cook for 2-3 minutes. Have a taste and adjust salt and pepper to your preference.
5. Add the chicken back in, and spoon the sauce over the chicken. Remove from heat. Garnish with chopped basil and extra parmesan if desired.

Nutrition facts:

Calories Per Serving 427; Total Fat: 32g; Sodium: 633mg; Total Carbs: 12g; Fiber: 1g; Sugars: 4g; Protein: 23g

Instant Pot Freezer Fix Chili

Servings: 6

Cooking Time: 35 Minutes

Ingredients:

- 1 lb frozen lean ground turkey
- 1 1/2 cup frozen corn (or 1 (15 oz) can kidney beans, rinsed)
- 1 (15-oz) can no-salt-added canned black beans (rinsed and drained)
- 1 (14.5 oz) can diced tomatoes with basil, garlic, and oregano
- 1 cup water
- 2 tbsp chili powder
- 1 tbsp cumin
- 1 1/2 tsp smoked paprika
- 3/4 tsp salt

Directions:

1. Place the frozen ground turkey in the pressure cooking pot. Top with the remaining ingredients.
2. Seal lid, close valve and set Manual button to 25 minutes. Use a quick pressure release.
3. When valve drops, carefully remove the lid and stir, breaking up turkey.

Nutrition facts:

Calories Per Serving 220; Total Fat: 7g; Sodium: 400mg; Total Carbs: 22g; Fiber: 5g; Sugars: 4g; Protein: 20g

Dijon Chicken W/ Zucchini & Tomatoes

Servings:4

Ingredients:

- 1 nonstick cooking spray
- 2 medium zucchini (cut into 1/4-inch rounds)
- 10 oz grape tomatoes
- 1 tbsp olive oil
- 1/4 tsp black pepper (ground, divided)
- 1/2 lemon (juiced)
- 2 tbsp Dijon Mustard
- 4 chicken breasts (4-ounce each, boneless, skinless)
- 1/2 tsp salt (optional)
- 1/2 tsp garlic powder
- 1 tsp dried oregano (dried)
- 1 tbsp Parmesan cheese (freshly grated)

Directions:

1. Preheat oven to 350 degrees. Coat a large baking dish with cooking spray. In a small bowl combine zucchini, tomatoes, olive oil, 1/8 Tsp. black pepper and toss to coat. Set aside.
2. In another small bowl mix together lemon juice and Dijon mustard. Set aside
3. Season chicken breasts on both sides with 1/8 Tsp. pepper, garlic powder and oregano. Place chicken breasts in baking dish and brush top with mustard mixture. Sprinkle with Parmesan cheese.
4. Pour zucchini and tomatoes around chicken in baking dish. Bake for 30 minutes or until done.

Nutrition facts:

Calories Per Serving 205; Total Fat: 7g; Sodium: 265mg; Total Carbs: 8g; Fiber: 2g; Protein: 27g

Brochetas (pinchos) De Albóndigas

Servings:6

Ingredients:

- 1/4 tsp pepper
- 24 grape or cherry tomatoes
- 2 tbsp Parmesan cheese (rallado)
- 8 oz fresh cremini mushrooms ((champiñones pequeños portabella), cortados a la mitad si es necesario para hacer 12 piezas)
- 1 medium onion (cortada a la mitad, luego en cuartos, luego cada cuarto en 3 (para un total de 12 piezas de cebolla))
- 20 oz lean ground turkey (93% sin grasa)
- 2 egg whites
- 1/4 cup balsamic vinegar
- 1 tsp olive oil
- 2 clove garlic (picado)
- 1/2 tsp salt (opcional)
- 12 bamboo skewers

Directions:

1. Precalienta el horno a 375°F (191°C). Cubre una charola con aceite en aerosol. Reserva.
2. Combina las claras de huevo, queso parmesano, ajo, pavo molido, sal (opcional), y pimienta. Mezcla bien y forma 12 albóndigas. Refrigera las albóndigas por al menos 30 minutos.
3. Ensarta 2 albóndigas, 2 tomates, 1 pieza de champiñón, y 1 pieza de cebolla alternando en cada brocheta.
4. En un tazón pequeño, bate el vinagre balsámico y el aceite de oliva.

5. Coloca las brochetas sobre la charola y cepilla las brochetas por todos los lados con el vinagre balsámico y la mezcla del aceite de oliva. Reserva el adobo.
6. Hornea las brochetas por unos 10 minutos. Frota todos los lados con la marinada de nuevo y hornea por unos 10-15 minutos adicionales. Las albóndigas deberían estar cocidas a una temperatura interna de al menos 165°F (73°C).

Nutrition facts:

Calories Per Serving 200; Total Fat: 8g; Sodium: 120mg; Total Carbs: 7g; Fiber: 1g; Sugars: 4g; Protein:0g

Easy Chicken Meatloaf

Servings:6

Cooking Time: 45 Minutes

Ingredients:
- 1 lbs 100% breast meat ground chicken
- 1/3 cup 100% whole grain bread crumbs
- 1 medium sweet onion, diced
- 1 tbs minced garlic
- 2 eggs
- 1/3 cup tomato paste (or ketchup)

Directions:
1. Mix all ingredients together in a large bowl.
2. Place the mix of ingredients in lightly greased casserole pan.
3. Bake at 400 F for 45 minutes or until chicken reaches internal temperature of 165 F.
4. Serve warm and enjoy!

Nutrition facts:

Calories Per Serving 157; Total Fat: 4g; Sodium: 159mg; Total Carbs: 12g; Fiber: 2g; Sugars: 5g; Protein: 10g

Baked Teriyaki Chicken

Servings:12

Cooking Time: 25 Minutes

Ingredients:
- 1 tbsp Cornstarch
- 1 tbsp cold water
- 1/2 cup Splenda® Granulated Sweetener
- 1/2 cup lower sodium soy sauce
- 1/4 cup Apple Cider Vinegar
- 1 clove garlic (minced)
- 1/2 tsp ground ginger
- 1/4 tsp black pepper
- 3 lbs boneless, skinless chicken breasts

Directions:
1. Preheat oven to 425°F. Spray a 13" x 9" baking dish with cooking spray.
2. In a saucepan, whisk together cornstarch and cold water until smooth. Whisk in Splenda Sweetener, soy sauce, vinegar, garlic, ginger, and pepper. Bring to a simmer over low heat and cook, stirring frequently, until sauce thickens and bubbles.
3. Place chicken in prepared baking dish and brush with teriyaki sauce. Turn chicken over, and brush again.
4. Bake for 15 minutes. Turn chicken and bake until chicken is no longer pink and juices run clear when pierced with the tip of a paring knife (20–30 minutes total baking time, depending on size). Brush with sauce every 10 minutes during baking.

Nutrition facts:

Calories Per Serving 170; Total Fat: 3.5g; Sodium: 440mg; Total Carbs: 3g; Fiber: 0g; Sugars: 1g; Protein: 30g

Air-fryer Turkey Croquettes

Servings: 6

Cooking Time: 10 Minutes

Ingredients:

- 2 cups mashed potatoes (with added milk and butter)
- 1/2 cup grated Parmesan cheese
- 1/2 cup shredded Swiss cheese
- 1 shallot, finely chopped
- 2 teaspoons minced fresh rosemary or 1/2 teaspoon dried rosemary, crushed
- 1 teaspoon minced fresh sage or 1/4 teaspoon dried sage leaves
- 1/2 teaspoon salt
- 1/4 teaspoon pepper
- 3 cups finely chopped cooked turkey
- 1 large egg
- 2 tablespoons water
- 1-1/4 cups panko bread crumbs
- Butter-flavored cooking spray
- Sour cream, optional

Directions:

1. Preheat air fryer to 350°. In a large bowl, combine mashed potatoes, cheeses, shallot, rosemary, sage, salt and pepper; stir in turkey. Mix lightly but thoroughly. Shape into twelve 1-in.-thick patties.
2. In a shallow bowl, whisk egg and water. Place bread crumbs in another shallow bowl. Dip croquettes in egg mixture, then in bread crumbs, patting to help coating adhere.
3. Working in batches, place croquettes in a single layer on greased tray in air-fryer basket; spritz with cooking spray. Cook until golden brown, 4-5 minutes. Turn; spritz with cooking spray. Cook until golden brown; 4-5 minutes. If desired, serve with sour cream.

Nutrition facts:

Calories Per Serving 360; Total Fat: 12.5g; Sodium: 813mg; Total Carbs: 27.3g; Fiber: 1g; Sugars: 1.3g; Protein: 33.3g

Skillet Creamy Lemon Chicken With Cauliflower

Servings: 4

Cooking Time: 15 Minutes

Ingredients:

- 1 pound thin cut chicken breasts
- 1 teaspoon salt
- 1/4 teaspoon pepper
- 1 tablespoon unsalted butter
- 1 cup chicken bone broth (or chicken stock)
- 4 cloves garlic (minced)
- 4 cups cauliflower (rice or chopped small)
- 1 tablespoon fresh thyme
- 2 tablespoons heavy cream
- 1 tablespoon lemon juice
- fresh thyme (garnish, optional)

Directions:

1. Season both sides of the chicken with salt and pepper.
2. 1 pound thin cut chicken breasts,1 teaspoon salt,1/4 teaspoon pepper
3. Heat a large skillet over medium high heat. Add the butter, and then cook the chicken until golden brown, about 3-5 minutes. Flip the chicken and cook about 2-4 minutes, or until cooked through. The internal temperature of chicken should read 165°F when taken with a meat thermometer inserted into the thickest part. Remove the chicken to a plate and tent with foil to keep warm.
4. 1 tablespoon unsalted butter

5. Add the chicken stock, garlic, and cauliflower to the skillet and stir, scraping up any bits from the bottom of the pan. Continue to simmer until the cauliflower is just tender about 4-5 minutes.
6. 1 cup chicken bone broth,4 cloves garlic,4 cups cauliflower
7. Remove the skillet from the heat and stir in the thyme, heavy cream and lemon juice.
8. 1 tablespoon fresh thyme,2 tablespoons heavy cream,1 tablespoon lemon juice
9. Add chicken back to the pan, garnish with additional fresh thyme, and serve hot.
10. fresh thyme

Nutrition facts:

Calories Per Serving 222; Total Fat: 8g; Sodium: 771mg; Total Carbs: 7g; Fiber: 2g; Sugars: 2g; Protein: 28g

Extra Crispy Air Fryer Chicken Wings

Servings:1
Cooking Time: 20 Minutes

Ingredients:

- SCALE
- 1 pound Chicken Wings (I used all flat pieces)
- 2 tablespoons Berbere
- 2 tablespoons Olive Oil
- 1 teaspoon garlic powder
- Salt and pepper to taste

Directions:

1. In a ziplock bag combine chicken wings, olive oil, garlic powder, salt and Berbere together.
2. For better flavor, let them marinade overnight, but if you need them quickly 30 minutes will do the job.
3. Spray your air fryer tray with olive oil (or pam). This prevents the wings from sticking to the tray.
4. Air Fry them according to the manufacturer's instructions. My Gourmia 5qt takes about 20 minutes on 400 degrees to reach 165 degrees.
5. Plate, and enjoy!

Nutrition facts:

Calories Per Serving 1147; Total Fat: 61.8g; Sodium: 2851mg; Total Carbs: 9.9g; Fiber: 0.3g; Sugars: 0.7g; Protein: 132.9g

OTHER FAVORITE RECIPES

Air Fryer Shishito Peppers With Lemon Aioli

Servings: 4
Cooking Time: 4 Minutes

Ingredients:
- ½ lb shishito peppers
- 1 teaspoon avocado oil or other oil with a high smoke point
- Lemon Aioli
- ½ cup vegan mayonnaise, or your favourite mayo
- 2 tablespoon lemon juice, freshly squeezed
- 1 clove garlic, finely minced
- 1 tablespoon fresh parsley, finely chopped
- ¼ tsp each sea salt and pepper

Directions:
1. Combine all ingredients for the Lemon Aioli in a small bowl. Set aside to allow flavours to blend.
2. Preheat the air fryer to 390°F. for 3 minutes.
3. Toss shishito peppers with oil, then add to the basket of the air fryer in a single layer.
4. Fry for 4 minutes. Push pause and check for doneness. Peppers should be slightly softened and lightly blistered. If not done, cook for another minute or two.
5. Remove to a serving dish, squeeze a little fresh lemon juice over all and sprinkle with sea salt. Serve with Lemon Aioli.

Nutrition facts:
Calories Per Serving: 220; Total Fat: 22g; Sodium: 367mg; Total Carbs: 5g; Fiber: 2g; Sugars: 3g; Protein: 1g

4-layer Stuffed Avocado

Servings: 4

Ingredients:
- 1/3 cup black beans (drained and rinsed)
- 2 avocados
- 4 tbsp Plain Nonfat Greek yogurt
- 4 tbsp salsa
- 4 tsp reduced-fat shredded cheddar or Mexican-style cheese
- 1/4 tsp salt
- 1 lime (quartered)

Directions:
1. Place the beans in a small bowl. Using the back of a fork, mash until they reach an almost smooth consistency.
2. Cut avocados in half and remove the pits. In the center of each avocado, layer 1 tablespoon of the beans, 1 tablespoon of Greek yogurt, and 1 tablespoon of salsa and sprinkle with 1 teaspoon of cheese. Sprinkle the salt evenly over the avocados. Serve each avocado half with 1 slice of lime to squeeze over the dish.

Nutrition facts:
Calories Per Serving 160; Total Fat: 12g; Sodium: 180mg; Total Carbs: 12g; Fiber: 6g; Sugars: 2g; Protein: 5g

Air-fryer French Toast Sticks

Servings:4

Ingredients:
- 4 large eggs
- ¾ cup whole milk
- 2 tablespoons granulated sugar
- 1 teaspoon vanilla extract
- 8 slices whole-wheat sandwich bread
- Cooking spray

Directions:
1. Whisk eggs, milk, sugar and vanilla together in a wide shallow dish. Cut bread slices into thirds lengthwise (24 pieces total).
2. Preheat air fryer to 325°F for 3 minutes. Lightly coat the basket with cooking spray. Working in batches, dip 8 bread sticks in the egg mixture, flipping constantly, until completely soaked, about 15 seconds. Arrange the soaked bread sticks in an even layer in the prepared basket; coat with cooking spray. Cook, flipping and coating with additional cooking spray halfway, until golden brown and interior is no longer wet, about 10 minutes. Transfer to a platter and cover with foil to keep warm. Repeat the process 2 more times with the remaining bread sticks and egg mixture.

Nutrition facts:
Calories Per Serving 278; Total Fat:8 g; Sodium: 301mg; Total Carbs: 37g; Fiber: 4g; Sugars: 6g; Protein: 15g

Brazilian Guacamole

Servings:13

Ingredients:
- 1 tbsp lower sodium soy sauce
- 1/2 tsp black pepper
- 1/2 cup olive oil
- 2 ripe Hass avocados
- 1/4 cup fresh cilantro (chopped)
- 1/4 cup fresh parsley (chopped)
- 1 clove garlic (finely minced)
- 1 green onion (scallion) (chopped)
- 1/2 yellow bell pepper (finely diced)
- 1/2 red bell pepper (finely diced)
- 1/2 English cucumber (peeled, seeded, and finely diced)
- 1 plum tomato (seeded and finely diced)
- 1/2 tsp salt

Directions:
1. Cut the avocados in half, remove the pits and scoop the flesh out of their shells. Dice or mash the avocado and add it to the vegetables. Slowly add the olive oil and fold everything together.
2. Combine the garlic, scallions, red onion, bell peppers, cucumber and tomato and toss well. Season with the soy sauce, salt and pepper, parsley and clinatro and fold well.
3. Refrigerate for at least 3 hours so that flavors can develop but remove from the fridge at least 20 minutes before serving.Tip: Cut the other half of the bell peppers and cucumber into sticks to serve with the guacamole for dipping

Nutrition facts:
Calories Per Serving 110; Total Fat: 10g; Sodium: 135mg; Total Carbs: 5g; Fiber: 2g; Sugars: 1g; Protein: 1g

Watermelon Gazpacho

Servings: 6

Ingredients:

- 4 cup seedless watermelon (cubed)
- 1 cucumber(s) (peeled and seeded)
- 1/2 red bell pepper (chopped)
- 4 med tomatoes (cored, seeds and membranes removed)
- 1/2 shallots (chopped)
- 1 small jalapeño pepper (trimmed and seeded)
- 1 tbsp sherry vinegar
- 1/4 cup olive oil
- 1/2 tsp salt
- 1/8 tsp black pepper
- 1/4 cup fresh basil (julienned)

Directions:

1. Refrigerate the gazpacho for at least an hour before serving.
2. To serve, divide gazpacho between bowls and top with basil. If desired, add a small drizzle of olive oil.
3. Place watermelon, cucumber, bell pepper, tomatoes, shallot, jalapeño, vinegar, olive oil, salt, and pepper in a blender. Blend until completely smooth. Taste and adjust seasonings if needed.

Nutrition facts:

Calories Per Serving 220; Total Fat: 18g; Sodium: 200mg; Total Carbs: 14g; Fiber: 2g; Sugars: 10g; Protein: 2g

Corn And Cheese Phyllo Empanadas

Servings: 8
Cooking Time: 30 Minutes

Ingredients:

- 1 tbsp olive oil
- 1 onion (finely chopped)
- 1 cup fresh, frozen, or canned corn kernels (thawed if frozen)
- 1/4 cup roasted red peppers (drained and thinly sliced)
- 2 green onion (scallion) (thinly sliced)
- 1/4 cup low-fat half-and-half
- 1/2 cup part-skim shredded mozzarella cheese
- 1 nonstick olive oil spray
- 8 (9x14-inch) sheets frozen phyllo dough (at room temperature)

Directions:

1. Heat the oil in a large nonstick skillet over medium-high heat. Add the onion and cook, stirring occasionally, until the onion is softened, about 6 minutes. Add the corn, roasted red peppers, and scallions; cook 2 minutes. Add the half-andhalf, stirring, until the liquid is almost evaporated, about 2 minutes. Remove from the heat; stir in the cheese. Let cool slightly.
2. Preheat the oven to 375°F. Spray a large baking sheet with nonstick spray.
3. Place one sheet of phyllo lengthwise on a work surface (cover the remaining phyllo with plastic wrap to keep from drying out). Lightly spray the phyllo sheet with nonstick spray; top with a second phyllo sheet and lightly spray with nonstick spray. With a sharp knife, cut the layered sheets in half

lengthwise. Repeat this layering and cutting process with the remaining phyllo sheets to make a total of 8 strips of dough.

4. Place a heaping Tbsp of filling to the left on the bottom end of one strip of phyllo. Fold one corner of the phyllo strip up and over the filling, then continue folding and overlapping, flag-fashion, to form a triangle. Place on the baking sheet and repeat with the remaining phyllo sheets and filling to make a total of 8 empanadas.
5. Lightly spray the empanadas with nonstick spray. Bake until the empanadas are golden brown, 15–20 minutes. Let cool 10 minutes before serving.

Nutrition facts:
Calories Per Serving 100; Total Fat: 4g; Sodium: 105mg; Total Carbs: 14g; Fiber: 1g; Sugars: 2g; Protein: 4g

Instant Pot Asian Spaghetti Squash

Servings: 6
Cooking Time: 17 Minutes

Ingredients:
- 1 (about 3 lbs) spaghetti squash
- 1 cup water
- 3 tbsp lower sodium soy sauce
- 2 limes
- 4 tsp sugar
- 1 tbsp grated fresh ginger
- 1/8 tsp crushed red pepper flakes
- 12 oz frozen shelled edamame
- 1 cup matchstick carrots
- 1/2 cup chopped green onion
- 2 oz unsalted peanuts or slivered almonds (chopped)
- 1/2 cup chopped fresh cilantro

Directions:
1. Pierce the squash over the entire surface with the tip of a sharp knife. Place in the microwave and set on high for 2 minutes. Using 2 dish towels or pot holders, carefully remove the squash from the microwave (it will be hot). Cut the squash in half crosswise, not lengthwise. Scrape out the seeds and connecting strands with a spoon.
2. Place the water and a trivet in the Instant Pot. Place the 2 squash halves on the trivet. Seal the lid, close the valve, and set the Manual/Pressure Cook button to 7 minutes.
3. Use a quick pressure release. Meanwhile, combine the soy sauce, juice of 1 of the limes, sugar, ginger, and crushed pepper flakes in a small bowl. Whisk until well blended and set aside.
4. When the valve drops, carefully remove the lid. Remove the squash halves and place on a cutting board. Remove the trivet.
5. Press the Cancel button and set to Sauté. Then press the Adjust button to "More" or "High." Add the edamame to the water, bring to a boil, and boil for 2 minutes. Drain well.
6. To create long spaghetti squash strands, run a fork around the outer edges of the squash to release the strands, rather than "raking through" the strands.
7. Place the squash in a large serving bowl or divide among 6 individual bowls. Top the squash evenly with the edamame, carrots, and green onion, spoon the soy sauce mixture evenly over all, and sprinkle with the nuts and cilantro. Do not stir. Cut the remaining lime into 6 wedges and serve with the squash to squeeze over all.

Nutrition facts:

Calories Per Serving 180; Total Fat: 8g; Sodium: 320mg; Total Carbs: 21g; Fiber: 6g; Sugars: 9g; Protein: 10g

Japanese Cucumber Salad

Servings:2

Ingredients:
- 1 medium cucumber
- 2 tbsp rice vinegar
- 1 tbsp olive oil
- 1 tsp honey or 1/2 packet artificial sweetener
- 1/4 tsp salt
- 1 tbsp sesame seeds (toasted)

Directions:
1. Peel the cucumbers to leave alternating green stripes. Slice the cucumbers in half lengthwise and scrape the seeds out with a spoon.
2. Using a mandolin, food processor, or knife, slice the cucumber into very thin slices.
3. In a medium bowl, whisk together the vinegar, canola oil, Splenda or Stevia, and salt (optional).
4. Toss the cucumbers and sesame seeds in the dressing and serve.

Nutrition facts:
Calories Per Serving 120; Total Fat: 9g; Sodium: 290mg; Total Carbs: 8g; Fiber: 1g; Sugars: 5g; Protein: 1g

Loaded Sheet-pan Nachos

Servings:12

Ingredients:
- 2 teaspoons extra-virgin olive oil
- 1 medium green bell pepper, diced
- 1 medium red onion, diced
- ½ teaspoon salt
- 1 (13 ounce) package tortilla chips
- 1 (8 ounce) package shredded Mexican blend or Cheddar cheese
- ¼ cup pickled jalapeños, chopped (Optional)
- ¼ cup sliced scallions
- ¼ cup roughly chopped fresh cilantro
- 1 medium avocado, diced
- Salsa verde and sour cream for serving

Directions:
1. Preheat oven to 400 degrees F.
2. Heat oil in a large skillet over medium heat. Add bell pepper, onion and salt; cook, stirring, until just tender, about 3 minutes.
3. Layer half the chips in a single layer on a sheet pan. Top with about half of the cooked vegetables and about 1/3 of the cheese.
4. Scatter the remaining chips on top of the first layer. Sprinkle with the remaining cooked vegetables, cheese and jalapeños (if using). Bake until the cheese is melted and just starting to turn golden brown, 8 to 10 minutes.
5. Top with scallions, cilantro and avocado. Serve with salsa and sour cream, if desired.

Nutrition facts:
Calories Per Serving 260; Total Fat: 16g; Sodium: 293mg; Total Carbs: 24g; Fiber: 3g; Sugars: 1g; Protein: 7g

Instant Pot Lentils And Poached Eggs

Servings:4

Cooking Time: 19 Minutes

Ingredients:

- 3/4 cup dried green or brown lentils (rinsed and drained)
- 2 bay leaves
- 3 cup water (divided)
- 3 tbsp olive oil
- 1 grated zest and juice of 1 lemon
- 1 tbsp finely chopped fresh parsley
- 1/2 tsp salt (divided)
- 1 nonstick cooking spray
- 4 eggs
- 4 cup baby spinach
- 1/4 tsp black pepper

Directions:

1. Place the lentils, bay leaves, and 2 cups of the water in the Instant Pot. Seal the lid, close the valve, and set the Manual/Pressure Cook button to 7 minutes.
2. Meanwhile, in a small bowl, whisk together the oil, parsley, lemon zest and juice, and 1/4 tsp of the salt. Set aside.
3. Coat 4 (6-oz) ramekins with cooking spray and crack 1 egg into each ramekin. Set aside.
4. Use a quick pressure release. When the valve drops, carefully remove the lid and drain the lentils, (discarding the lentil water and 2 bay leaves). Return the lentils to the Instant Pot with the spinach and 1/4 tsp of the salt. Toss until the spinach is just wilted and divide it between 4 soup bowls. Cover to keep warm.
5. Add 1 cup of water to the pot, add a trivet and 3 ramekins. Stack the 4th ramekin on top of the other ramekins. Seal the lid, close the valve, press the Cancel button, and reset the Manual/Pressure Cook button to 1 minute.
6. Use a natural pressure release for 1 minute, followed by a quick pressure release. When the valve drops, carefully remove the lid. Remove the ramekins and drain off any excess water that may have accumulated while cooking. Carefully run a knife around outer edges of each egg to release from the ramekin easily.
7. Spoon equal amounts of the oil mixture on top of each serving of lentils and top with the eggs. Sprinkle with black pepper.

Nutrition facts:

Calories Per Serving 280; Total Fat: 15g; Sodium: 390mg; Total Carbs: 22g; Fiber: 9g; Sugars: 2g; Protein: 16g

Sweet Potato-black Bean Burgers

Servings:4

Ingredients:

- 2 cups grated sweet potato
- ½ cup old-fashioned rolled oats
- 1 cup no-salt-added black beans, rinsed
- ½ cup chopped scallions
- ¼ cup vegan mayonnaise
- 1 tablespoon no-salt-added tomato paste
- 1 teaspoon curry powder
- ⅛ teaspoon salt
- 1/2 cup plain unsweetened almond milk yogurt
- 2 tablespoons chopped fresh dill
- 2 tablespoons lemon juice

- 2 tablespoons extra-virgin olive oil
- 4 whole-wheat hamburger buns, toasted
- 1 cup thinly sliced cucumber

Directions:

1. Squeeze grated sweet potato with paper towels to remove excess moisture; place in a large bowl. Pulse oats in a food processor until finely ground; add to the bowl with the sweet potatoes. Add beans, scallions, mayonnaise, tomato paste, curry powder and salt to the bowl; mash the mixture together with your hands. Shape into four 1/2-inch-thick patties. Place the patties on a plate; refrigerate for 30 minutes.
2. Stir yogurt, dill and lemon juice together in a small bowl; set aside.
3. Heat oil in a large cast-iron skillet over medium-high heat. Add the patties; cook until golden brown, about 3 minutes per side.
4. Divide the yogurt sauce evenly among top and bottom bun halves. Top each bottom bun half with a burger and cucumber slices; replace top bun halves.

Nutrition facts:

Calories Per Serving454; Total Fat: 22g; Sodium: 432mg; Total Carbs: 54g; Fiber: 9g; Sugars: 9g; Protein:12 g

Air-fryer Jalapeño Poppers

Servings:4

Ingredients:

- 2 ounces cream cheese, softened
- ¼ cup finely chopped cooked chicken breast (about 1 1/4 oz.)
- ¼ cup finely shredded sharp Cheddar cheese (1 oz.)
- ¼ cup finely chopped scallion
- 2 tablespoons hot sauce
- 2 teaspoons chopped fresh dill
- 4 large jalapeño peppers, halved lengthwise (about 1 1/2 oz. each)
- 2 tablespoons whole-wheat panko breadcrumbs
- Cooking spray

Directions:

1. Combine cream cheese, chicken, Cheddar, scallion, hot sauce and dill in a medium bowl; stir until well combined. Clean seeds and membranes from jalapeños and stuff evenly with the cream cheese mixture. Sprinkle with breadcrumbs. Place the stuffed jalapeños in the basket of an air fryer; coat with cooking spray. Cook at 370 degrees F until the tops are browned and the jalapeños are tender, about 10 minutes.

Nutrition facts:

Calories Per Serving104; Total Fat: 8g; Sodium: 288mg; Total Carbs: 4g; Fiber: 1g; Sugars: 1g; Protein: 5g

Butternut Squash Queso Fundido

Servings:32

Ingredients:

- 1 medium butternut squash (about 2 1/4 pounds), halved and seeded
- ½ teaspoon salt
- 1 tablespoon extra-virgin olive oil
- 1 large sweet onion, sliced
- 1 tablespoon chili powder
- ¼ teaspoon chipotle chile powder or cayenne pepper
- 8 ounces sharp Cheddar cheese, shredded

- 8 ounces Monterey Jack cheese, shredded
- ⅔ cup pico de gallo or fresh salsa, drained
- 2 tablespoons chopped fresh cilantro
- 2 tablespoons toasted pepitas

Directions:

1. Preheat oven to 400 degrees F. Line a baking sheet with parchment paper.
2. Place squash cut-side down on the prepared pan. Bake until tender, 50 minutes to 1 hour. Turn over and let cool slightly. Scoop the flesh into a food processor and add salt. Puree until smooth. Measure out 2 cups of puree (reserve any remaining squash for another use). Set aside.
3. Meanwhile, combine oil and onion in a medium saucepan. Cover and cook over medium heat, stirring often, for 10 minutes. Uncover and continue cooking until the onion is very soft and browned, 8 to 10 minutes more, reducing the heat and adding 1 tablespoon water at a time, as needed, if the onion begins browning too quickly. Stir in chili powder and chipotle (or cayenne). Remove from heat, cover and let stand for 10 minutes.
4. When the squash is done, reduce oven temperature to 350 degrees. Coat a medium cast-iron skillet (10-inch) with cooking spray.
5. Toss Cheddar and Monterey Jack in a large bowl. Stir 1 cup of the cheeses into the reserved squash puree. Spread about half of the remaining cheese in the prepared pan. Top with the squash. Spread half of the caramelized onions over the squash. Top with the remaining cheese and onions.
6. Bake until the cheese is melted and bubbling along the edges, about 20 minutes. Let cool for 10 minutes. Top with pico de gallo (or salsa), cilantro and pepitas.

Nutrition facts:

Calories Per Serving107; Total Fat: 7g; Sodium: 212mg; Total Carbs: 7g; Fiber: 1g; Sugars: 2g; Protein:5 g

Chunky Black Bean Salsa With Corn & Bell Pepper

Servings:16

Ingredients:

- 2 teaspoons lime zest
- ¼ cup lime juice
- ¼ cup canola oil
- 1 tablespoon ground cumin
- 1 tablespoon honey
- ¾ teaspoon salt
- 2 (15 ounce) cans low-sodium black beans, rinsed
- 1 ½ cups fresh corn kernels (from 3 ears)
- 1 large red bell pepper, finely chopped
- 1 large tomato, chopped
- 1 medium red onion, finely chopped
- ¾ cup chopped fresh cilantro leaves
- 2 medium scallions, thinly sliced
- 1 large jalapeño pepper, finely chopped
- 1 (16-oz.) bag blue or yellow corn tortilla chips

Directions:

1. Whisk together lime zest, lime juice, oil, cumin, honey, and salt in a large bowl. Gently stir in beans, corn, bell pepper, tomato, red onion, cilantro, scallions and jalapeño. Cover and refrigerate for at least 30 minutes and up to 4 days.
2. Remove from refrigerator about 30 minutes before serving. Serve with tortilla chips.
3. To make ahead
4. Refrigerate for up to 4 days; the salsa will get more and more flavorful.

Nutrition facts:

Calories Per Serving 240; Total Fat: 11g; Sodium: 228mg; Total Carbs: 32g; Fiber: 5g; Sugars: 1g; Protein: 5g

Low Carb Baked Feta Rice

Servings:12

Cooking Time: 35 Minutes

Ingredients:

- 8 ounce block of feta (not crumbled)
- 2 pints cherry tomatoes
- 1/3 cup olive oil
- pinch of salt
- pinch of pepper
- 1 tsp minced garlic
- 1/4 cup fresh basil
- 2 bags Garlic Herb RightRice

Directions:

1. Preheat oven to 400 F. In a baking dish, add cherry tomatoes and drizzle ¼ cup olive oil over top. Season with salt and pepper and the toss lightly to combine.
2. Place the feta cheese block in the middle of the baking dish and surround it with the cherry tomatoes. Drizzle remaining olive oil over feta and tomatoes.
3. Bake for about 35 minutes or until cheese is melted and tomatoes are soft and bursting.
4. While tomatoes and cheese bake, prepare RightRice in a pot of water according to the package instructions.
5. Remove tomatoes from oven and add in garlic and basil. Toss to combine.
6. Add prepared rice to the baking dish and toss to combine. Garnish with basil as desired and serve warm.

Nutrition facts:

Calories Per Serving: 238; Total Fat: 11g; Sodium: 420mg; Total Carbs: 24g; Fiber: 4g; Sugars: 3g; Protein: 10g

Garbanzo Bean And Arugula Salad

Servings:4

Ingredients:

- 1/4 cup sundried tomatoes packed in olive oil and italian herbs (drained)
- 1 (15.5 oz) can chickpeas (garbanzo beans) (drained and rinsed)
- 2 cup fresh arugula
- 1 clove garlic (minced)

Directions:

1. Combine garbanzo beans, drained tomatoes, and garlic in a salad bowl.
2. Mix in arugula. Let sit for 10 minutes to slightly wilt the arugula leaves before serving.

Nutrition facts:

Calories Per Serving150; Total Fat:4.5g; Sodium:1 20mg; Total Carbs: 22g; Fiber: 6g; Sugars: 5g; Protein: 7g

SNACKS, APPETIZERS AND SIDERS RECIPES

Air-fryer Crispy Chickpeas

Servings: 4

Ingredients:
- 1 (15 ounce) can unsalted chickpeas, rinsed and drained
- 1 ½ tablespoons toasted sesame oil
- ¼ teaspoon smoked paprika
- ¼ teaspoon crushed red pepper
- ⅛ teaspoon salt
- Cooking spray
- 2 lime wedges

Directions:
1. Spread chickpeas on several layers of paper towels. Top with more paper towels and pat until very dry, rolling the chickpeas under the paper towels to dry all sides.
2. Combine the chickpeas and oil in a medium bowl. Sprinkle with paprika, crushed red pepper and salt. Pour into an air fryer basket and coat with cooking spray. Cook at 400 degrees F until very well browned, 12 to 14 minutes, shaking the basket occasionally. Squeeze lime wedges over the chickpeas and serve.

Nutrition facts:
Calories Per Serving 132; Total Fat: 6g; Sodium: 86mg; Total Carbs: 14g; Fiber: 3g; Protein: 5g

Air-fryer Cauliflower Gnocchi With Marinara Dipping Sauce

Servings: 8

Ingredients:
- 2 (10 ounce) packages frozen cauliflower gnocchi, thawed, divided
- 3 tablespoons extra-virgin olive oil, divided
- ½ cup grated Parmesan cheese, divided
- 2 tablespoons chopped fresh flat-leaf parsley
- 1 cup reduced-sodium marinara sauce, warmed

Directions:
1. Preheat air fryer to 375 degrees F. Toss 1 package gnocchi, 1 1/2 tablespoons oil and 2 tablespoons Parmesan together in a large bowl.
2. Coat the basket of the air fryer with cooking spray. Transfer the gnocchi mixture to the basket; cook for 5 minutes, turning once halfway through. Transfer to a large bowl. Repeat the procedure with the remaining gnocchi and oil and 2 tablespoons Parmesan. Sprinkle the cooked gnocchi with parsley and the remaining 1/4 cup Parmesan. Serve with marinara.

Nutrition facts:
Calories Per Serving 160; Total Fat: 9g; Sodium: 163mg; Total Carbs: 14g; Fiber: 4g; Sugars: 2g; Protein: 3 g

Easiest Air Fryer Kale Chips

Servings: 2
Cooking Time: 3 Minutes

Ingredients:
- 2 cups kale Use Curly kale. Wash the kale well.
- ½ teaspoon olive oil Avocado oil. Olive oil can be used instead, if needed.
- ¼ teaspoon salt Preferably coarse sea salt, but any salt will do.

Directions:
1. Remove the thick inner rib from each kale leaf.
2. Tear kale into pieces.
3. Place kale pieces in a single layer in an air fryer basket fit for your air fryer.
4. Lightly coat each piece with oil.
5. Sprinkle with salt.
6. Air fry at 325° for 3-4 minutes. If your air fryer is pre-heated, they probably won't take longer than 3 minutes, so keep a close eye on them.
7. Let cool to room temperature. Enjoy!

Nutrition facts:
Calories Per Serving 42; Total Fat: 2g; Sodium: 316mg; Total Carbs: 6g; Fiber: 0g; Sugars: 0g; Protein: 3g

Double-tahini Hummus

Servings:16

Ingredients:
- 8 ounces dried chickpeas (about 1 cup)
- 1 tablespoon baking soda
- 7 large cloves garlic, peeled
- ½ cup extra-virgin olive oil, divided
- 1/2 cup cold tahini (see Tip), divided
- ¼ cup fresh lemon juice plus 1 tablespoon, divided
- 1 ½ teaspoons kosher salt
- ¼ teaspoon ground cumin, plus more for garnish
- Paprika for garnish
- ¼ cup chopped flat-leaf parsley

Directions:
1. Place chickpeas in a medium saucepan and cover with 2 inches of water; stir in baking soda. Soak overnight. (Alternatively, to quick-soak: Bring the chickpea mixture in the saucepan to a boil. Boil for 2 minutes. Remove from heat, cover and let stand for 1 hour.)
2. Drain the chickpeas and rinse well. Rinse out the pan. Return the chickpeas to the pan and cover with 2 inches fresh water. Add garlic. Bring to a boil. Keep at a rolling boil until the chickpeas are tender and almost falling apart, 25 to 40 minutes.
3. Reserve about 3/4 cup of the cooking water, then drain the chickpeas. Set aside 2 tablespoons of the prettiest chickpeas for garnish. Rinse the remaining chickpeas and garlic and set the colander over a bowl. Refrigerate the chickpea mixture, reserved cooking water and pretty chickpeas separately overnight.
4. The next day, combine the chickpeas, 6 of the garlic cloves and 1/2 cup of the reserved cooking water in a food processor (or blender) with 1/4 cup each oil, tahini and 1/4 cup lemon juice, salt and cumin. Process until creamy. Transfer to a serving bowl. Puree the remaining 1/4 cup each oil and tahini with the remaining garlic clove, 2 table-spoons of the cooking water and 1 tablespoon lemon juice until smooth.
5. Make an indention in the center of the hummus and spoon in the tahini-lemon mixture. Sprinkle the hummus with cumin and paprika, if desired. Garnish with the reserved whole chickpeas and parsley.

Nutrition facts:
Calories Per Serving159; Total Fat:12 g; Sodium: 139mg; Total Carbs: 11g; Fiber: 3g; Sugars: 2g; Protein: 4g

Air-fryer Tofu Steaks

Servings:4
Cooking Time: 10 Minutes

Ingredients:
- 1/4 cup olive oil
- 3 tablespoons reduced-sodium soy sauce
- 2 green onions, chopped
- 2 garlic cloves, minced
- 1/4 teaspoon ground cumin
- 1/4 teaspoon crushed red pepper flakes
- 1 package (14 ounces) extra-firm tofu

Directions:
1. In a bowl or shallow dish, combine the first 6 ingredients. Cut tofu lengthwise into 3/8-in. thick slices; cut each slice in half diagonally to make triangles. Add to marinade and turn to coat. Refrigerate 3-5 hours, turning occasionally.
2. Preheat air fryer to 400°. Reserving marinade, place tofu on greased tray in air-fryer basket. Drizzle remaining marinade over tops. Cook until lightly browned and heated through, 6-8 minutes.

Nutrition facts:
Calories Per Serving 121; Total Fat: 12.7g; Sodium: 452mg; Total Carbs: 2.3g; Fiber: 0.4g; Sugars:0.4g; Protein: 1g

Crispy Garlic Keto Croutons Recipe Air Fryer

Servings:10
Cooking Time: 10 Minutes

Ingredients:
- 2 Cups of Keto Farmers Bread (200 grams) half of the loaf
- 1 Tablespoon of Marjoram
- 2Tablespoon Olive Oil
- 1/2 Tablespoon Garlic Powder

Directions:
1. As already mentioned, pick your favorite bread. Chop fresh herbs and get olive oil ready.
2. Make sure your bread is cooled. Cut it into same-size slices and subsequently squares. As you see in the image, I have made smaller bread cubes, as I always love everything in more minor variations. For me, it tastes better as big chunks.
3. Place all of the croutons into a large bowl. Add oil and all the ingredients, herbs of your choice, and a bit of salt and pepper. With a big spatula, mix all of the croutons thoroughly. Remember to make sure the oil and herbs are spread evenly.
4. Depending on your Air Fryer, fill it up with your croutons. Make sure you only add one layer. Otherwise, they will not crisp fully.
5. Switch the Air Fryer on. You do not need to add additional oil since you have already coated your croutons with oil.
6. After 10 minutes, the crunchy croutons are golden brown and ready to be served. Let them cool or serve them still hot or warm. It all depends on how you want to use them.

Nutrition facts:
Calories Per Serving 50; Total Fat: 4g; Sodium: 0mg; Total Carbs: 1g; Fiber: 4g; Sugars: 0g; Protein: 2g

Air Fryer Pumpkin Seeds

Servings:7
Cooking Time: 15 Minutes

Ingredients:
- 1 ¾ cup whole raw pumpkin seeds
- 1 tablespoon olive oil
- ¼ teaspoon salt
- ¼ teaspoon garlic powder

Directions:
1. Remove the seeds from the pumpkin. Place in a strainer and run cold water over the seeds, removing any pieces of orange stringy stuff. (Run your hands through the seeds several times as this will help break up any orange stringy stuff so that you can remove it.)
2. Place the cleaned pumpkin seeds on a paper towel lined plate. Use another double-layered paper towel to press on top of the seeds, helping to dry them.
3. Once mostly dry, place the pumpkin seeds in a medium mixing bowl. Shake the paper towels over the bowl if needed to remove any seeds that have stuck to them.
4. Add the olive oil, salt, and garlic powder to the bowl with the pumpkin seeds. Give everything a good stir, then pour the seeds into the air fryer basket.
5. Air fry at 350 degrees F for 15 minutes, shaking the basket once halfway through. When done, the seeds should be a light golden-brown color and crispy. Let cool before eating.
6. Store roasted pumpkin seeds in an airtight container at room temperature for up to a week.

Nutrition facts:
Calories Per Serving 187; Total Fat: 16.5g; Sodium: 90mg; Total Carbs: 4.5g; Fiber: 2g; Sugars: 0g; Protein: 9g

Air Fryer Tofu

Servings:4
Cooking Time: 10 Minutes

Ingredients:
- 350 grams (12 ounce) block extra firm tofu GMO free preferred
- 2 tablespoons tamari or soy sauce if not avoiding gluten
- 1 tablespoon rice vinegar
- 1 tablespoon cornstarch
- 1 teaspoon garlic powder
- 1 teaspoon onion powder
- 1 teaspoon smoked paprika or sweet
- 1/4 teaspoon sea salt optional

Directions:
1. Press the Tofu
2. Cut your tofu into half inch cubes. Then arrange some paper towels or a clean dish towel on a cutting board and place the tofu cubes in a single layer on top. Now add more paper towels on top of the cubes and place another cutting board, flat plate or baking sheet on top. Finally place something very heavy on top like a cast iron skillet or a heavy book. Press like this for 15 minutes while you prepare the remaining ingredients.
3. Prepare the Tofu

4. Combine all the dry seasoning, including the corn starch in a small bowl, and set aside.
5. Place the pressed tofu cubes in a shallow dish or container and pour the tamari and rice vinegar on top, toss to evenly coat. Then sprinkle all the seasoning on top and mix well. If you use a container, you can put the lid on and gently rotate the container around to evenly spread the seasoning.
6. Arrange your cubes in your fryer basket in a single layer working in two batches, if you have a small fryer. Do not over crowd your tofu to ensure maximum crispiness. Air fry at 400 degrees F for 10-15 minutes, mixing or shaking your basket around the halfway point. Mine were perfect at 13 minutes, but start checking on the tofu around the 10 minute mark.
7. Serve with a dip like spicy mayo or cashew cream. Or use to top some rice and veggies.

Nutrition facts:
Calories Per Serving67; Total Fat: 2g; Sodium: 559mg; Total Carbs: 5g; Fiber: 1g; Sugars: 1g; Protein: 8g

Avocado Fries With Sriracha Aioli

Servings:8

Ingredients:
- Cooking spray
- 2 firm avocados, cut into 1/2-inch-thick wedges
- ½ teaspoon salt
- ¼ teaspoon ground pepper
- ⅓ cup white whole-wheat flour
- 2 large eggs, lightly beaten
- 1 cup whole-wheat panko breadcrumbs
- ⅓ cup mayonnaise
- 2 tablespoons Sriracha

Directions:
1. Preheat oven to 425 degrees F. Coat a large rimmed baking sheet with cooking spray.
2. Season avocados with salt and pepper. Place flour, eggs and panko in 3 separate shallow dishes. Coat the avocado wedges in the flour, then dip in the egg. Coat both sides with the panko, pressing to help it stick. Place the wedges on the prepared baking sheet. Coat both sides with cooking spray.
3. Bake until golden brown, turning halfway through, 25 to 30 minutes.
4. Whisk mayonnaise and Sriracha in a small bowl. Serve the avocado fries with the aioli.

Nutrition facts:
Calories Per Serving221; Total Fat: 18g; Sodium: 280mg; Total Carbs: 14g; Fiber: 4g; Sugars: 1g; Protein:3 g

Perfectly Roasted Air Fryer Sweet Potato Chunks

Servings:4
Cooking Time: 8 Minutes

Ingredients:
- 1 sweet potato One large sweet potato or two smaller ones (about two cups when cut into pieces)
- 2 teaspoon olive oil extra virgin
- 1 pinch salt
- 1 dash cayenne pepper optional

Directions:
1. Scrub sweet potato well.
2. Cut sweet potato into small chunks. See notes.
3. Place sweet potato chunks into a bowl and toss to coat.
4. Spread sweet potato pieces out in a single layer on the air fryer rack fit for your air fryer.
5. Sprinkle salt on top of the sweet potatoes. If your kids like spicey food, top sweet potatoes with just a dash of cayenne pepper.
6. Air fry at 400°F for 8 minutes.
7. Serve and enjoy!

Nutrition facts:
Calories Per Serving 66; Total Fat: 2g; Sodium: 41mg; Total Carbs: 11g; Fiber: 2g; Sugars: 2g; Protein: 1g

Air-fryer Blooming Onions

Servings: 8

Ingredients:
- Cooking spray
- 2 large (12-ounce) sweet onions
- 2 large eggs
- ½ cup low-fat milk
- ¼ cup whole-wheat flour
- 1 teaspoon paprika, divided
- ½ teaspoon garlic powder
- ½ teaspoon onion powder
- ½ teaspoon salt, divided
- ¼ teaspoon cayenne pepper, divided
- 1 cup panko breadcrumbs
- ½ cup mayonnaise
- 2 tablespoons cocktail sauce

Directions:
1. Preheat air fryer to 375°F for 5 minutes. Coat the fryer basket with cooking spray.
2. Trim stem end off onions and peel the onions (leaving roots intact). Place the onions, root-sides down, on a cutting board and cut down through each onion, stopping 1/4 inch above the roots, to create 16 sections.
3. Whisk eggs, milk, flour, 1/2 teaspoon paprika, garlic powder, onion powder, 1/4 teaspoon salt and 1/8 teaspoon cayenne in a medium bowl. Place breadcrumbs in another medium bowl.
4. Dip each onion into the batter, allowing excess to drip off, then dredge in the breadcrumbs to coat completely. (Pull the onion "petals" apart often during the dredging process to make sure you are getting batter and breadcrumbs into every nook and cranny.) Place the onions in the prepared basket and coat with cooking spray. Cook until crispy, 20 to 25 minutes. Sprinkle with the remaining 1/4 teaspoon salt.
5. Meanwhile, whisk mayonnaise, cocktail sauce and the remaining 1/2 teaspoon paprika and 1/8 teaspoon cayenne in a small bowl. Serve the onions with the dipping sauce.

Nutrition facts:
Calories Per Serving170; Total Fat: 11g; Sodium: 264mg; Total Carbs: 15g; Fiber: 1g; Sugars: 5g; Protein: 3g

Sweet Potato Skins With Guacamole

Servings: 8

Ingredients:
- Potato Skins
- 4 small sweet potatoes
- 1 tablespoon extra-virgin olive oil
- ⅛ teaspoon kosher salt
- ½ cup shredded Cheddar cheese
- Guacamole & Toppings
- 1 ripe avocado
- 1 tablespoon lime juice
- 1 clove garlic, minced
- ⅛ teaspoon salt
- ¼ cup chopped tomato
- 2 tablespoons minced red onion
- Chopped cilantro for garnish

Directions:
1. Preheat oven to 400 degrees F.
2. Tightly wrap sweet potatoes in foil and place on a baking sheet. Roast until very tender, 50 minutes to 1 hour. Carefully unwrap and set aside to cool.
3. Line a baking sheet with parchment paper.
4. Cut the potatoes in half lengthwise and scoop out the flesh, leaving a 1/4-inch border (save the scooped-out flesh for another use). Place the sweet potato halves skin-side up on the prepared baking sheet. Brush with oil and sprinkle with kosher salt. Bake until browned and crisp, 20 to 30 minutes.
5. Cut each skin in half widthwise and return to the baking sheet, skin-side down. Sprinkle each with 1 tablespoon Cheddar. Return to the oven and bake until the cheese is melted, 8 to 10 minutes.
6. Meanwhile, make the guacamole: Mash avocado in a medium bowl. Stir in lime juice, garlic and salt.
7. Top each sweet potato skin with guacamole, tomato, onion and cilantro, if desired.

Nutrition facts:
Calories Per Serving117; Total Fat: 8g; Sodium: 113mg; Total Carbs: 10g; Fiber: 3g; Sugars: 3g; Protein: 3g

Keto Fried Pickles

Servings: 4
Cooking Time: 12 Minutes

Ingredients:
- 2 eggs
- 3 dill pickles sliced
- 1/2 cup almond flour
- 1/4 cup grated parmesan cheese
- 1 tsp salt

Directions:
1. Spray Air Fryer with non stick cooking spray.
2. Pour eggs in a bowl.
3. In a separate shallow bowl, combine almond flour, Parmesan cheese, and salt.
4. Spray Air Fryer basket with non stick cooking spray.
5. Dip sliced pickles in eggs, then in almond flour mixture and line in Air Fryer.
6. Repeat until Air Fryer basket is filled.
7. Spray with non stick cooking spray.
8. Cook at 360 degrees for 5 minutes. Open basket. Flip.
9. Cook for an additional 5-7 minutes.

Nutrition facts:
Calories Per Serving 143; Total Fat: 11g; Sodium: 1135mg; Total Carbs: 5g; Fiber: 2g; Sugars: 1g; Protein: 8g

Garlic Parmesan Kale Chips

Servings: 2
Cooking Time: 10 Minutes

Ingredients:
- 5 ounces raw kale, washed and dried (about 6 cups) tough stems removed, if desired. Use bagged, chopped kale if desired.
- 1 tablespoon olive oil
- 1/4 teaspoon sea salt
- 1/4 teaspoon garlic powder
- 1 tablespoon grated Parmesan cheese or more to taste

Directions:
1. If you're using whole kale leaves, chop or slice the kale into about 2-inch pieces.
2. Place the kale in a mixing bowl. Pour the olive oil over, and sprinkle with salt and garlic powder.
3. Gently toss the kale and massage the salt and garlic powder into the kale. Make sure everything is coated with the oil.
4. Place the kale into the air fryer basket. Set the temperature to 300 °F, and the timer for 9 minutes.
5. Open the air fryer and toss the kale with tongs after about 5 minutes. Check it as it gets close to the finishing point, to make sure it's not overcooked.
6. Empty the cooked kale chips into the mixing bowl, sprinkle with Parmesan cheese, and let cool for about 2 minutes.

Nutrition facts:
Calories Per Serving 109; Total Fat: 8g; Sodium: 356mg; Total Carbs: 7g; Fiber: 1g; Sugars: 1g; Protein: 4g

Better Mashed Potatoes

Servings: 10
Cooking Time: 15 Minutes

Ingredients:
- 1/3 cup low-fat buttermilk
- 1 head cauliflower (separated into small florets, discard core and stem)
- 5 clove garlic (peeled and left whole)
- 1 brusset or baking potato (peeled and cut into 2-inch cubes)
- 1 tbsp olive oil
- 2 tsp butter (unsalted butter)
- 2 tbsp Parmesan cheese (grated)
- 1 tsp salt
- 1/2 tsp black pepper

Directions:
1. In a large saucepan, place the potato, garlic, and cauliflower and enough water to cover. Bring to boiling, reduce the heat to medium, and cook until the potato and cauliflower are tender, about 15 minutes.
2. Drain and add the vegetables and garlic back to the pot. Cover the pot with a kitchen towel and put the lid over the towel. Let stand for 5 minutes. Remove the lid and towel. This process helps to dry the vegetables so they mash better.

3. Add the buttermilk, cheese, olive oil, butter, salt, and pepper. Mash* just until the ingredients are lightly combined. If desired, garnish with fresh snipped chives.

Nutrition facts:
Calories Per Serving60; Total Fat: 2g; Sodium: 230mg; Total Carbs: 7g; Fiber: 2g; Sugars: 2g; Protein: 2g

Roasted Buffalo Chickpeas

Servings:4

Ingredients:
- 1 tablespoon white vinegar
- ½ teaspoon cayenne pepper, or to taste
- ¼ teaspoon salt
- 1 (15 ounce) can no-salt-added chickpeas, rinsed

Directions:
1. Position rack in upper third of oven; preheat to 400 degrees F.
2. Combine vinegar, cayenne and salt in a large bowl. Very thoroughly pat chickpeas dry, then toss with the vinegar mixture. Spread on a rimmed baking sheet. Roast the chickpeas, stirring twice, until browned and crunchy, 30 to 35 minutes. Let cool on the pan for 30 minutes; the chickpeas will crisp as they cool.

Nutrition facts:
Calories Per Serving109; Total Fat: 1g; Sodium: 162mg; Total Carbs: 18g; Fiber: 4g; Protein: 6g

Air Fryer Crispy Bacon

Servings:5
Cooking Time: 8 Minutes

Ingredients:
- 5 strips bacon

Directions:
1. Add bacon into preheated to 375 degrees air fryer basket. Try to put it in one layer
2. Cook for 8 minutes, checking couple time to make sure to achieve the desired level of crispiness.
3. Serve with eggs!

Nutrition facts:
Calories Per Serving 91; Total Fat: 8g; Sodium: 145mg; Total Carbs: 0g; Fiber: 0g; Sugars: 0g; Protein: 43g

Loaded Sheet-pan NachosOven-fried Pickles

Servings:8

Ingredients:
- 8 ounces sliced dill pickles (about 1 1/3 cups)
- 1 cup whole-wheat panko breadcrumbs
- ⅓ cup all-purpose flour
- 2 eggs, lightly beaten
- Cooking spray
- ½ cup sour cream
- 1 tablespoon chopped fresh dill
- 1 teaspoon dried minced garlic
- 1 teaspoon lemon juice
- ¼ teaspoon salt, divided

Directions:
1. Preheat oven to 425 degrees F. Set a wire rack on a rimmed baking sheet and coat with cooking spray.
2. Pat pickle slices dry. Place panko, flour and eggs in three separate shallow dishes. Working in batches, dredge the pickles in the flour, coat with the egg and then the panko, patting the crumbs to adhere. Place on the prepared rack. Coat liberally with cooking spray. Bake until crisp and beginning to brown, about 10 minutes.
3. Meanwhile, combine sour cream, dill, dried garlic, lemon juice and 1/8 teaspoon salt in a small bowl.
4. To serve, transfer the pickles to a platter and sprinkle with the remaining 1/8 teaspoon salt. Serve with the sauce.

Nutrition facts:
Calories Per Serving 89; Total Fat: 5g; Sodium: 328mg; Total Carbs:9 g; Fiber: 1g; Sugars: 1g; Protein: 3g

Make Egg Rolls In The Air Fryer For A High-fiber Appetizer That Everyone Will Love

Servings:3

Ingredients:
- 1 teaspoon canola oil
- 5 ounces ground pork
- 2 teaspoons finely chopped garlic
- 3 cups finely sliced green cabbage (about 6 oz.)
- ¼ cup chopped scallions
- 1 tablespoon lime juice
- 1 teaspoon reduced-sodium soy sauce
- 6 egg roll wrappers
- 1 large egg, well beaten
- Cooking spray

Directions:
1. Heat oil in a medium skillet over medium-high heat. Add pork and garlic; cook until well browned, about 3 minutes, stirring occasionally. Add cabbage and scallions; cook, stirring occasionally, until the cabbage is starting to wilt, about 3 minutes. Stir in lime juice and soy sauce. Remove from heat.
2. Lay out 3 egg roll wrappers with 1 point away from you; brush 1 side completely with egg. Place 3-4 tablespoons of the filling in the center of each wrapper. Roll the point closest to you over the filling; then bring the side points into the middle. Continue rolling away from you to form a tight seal around the filling. Repeat the process with the remaining wraps and filling.
3. Place the egg rolls in the basket of an air fryer and coat with cooking spray. Cook at 390°F until golden brown, about 10 minutes, turning halfway through.

Nutrition facts:
Calories Per Serving315; Total Fat:7 g; Sodium: 508mg; Total Carbs: 43g; Fiber: 3g; Sugars: 3g; Protein: 19g

Crispy Parmesan Mushroom Fries With Ranch Sauce

Servings:6

Ingredients:
- Cooking spray
- 4 large portobello mushrooms or portobello caps
- ½ cup all-purpose flour
- 3 large egg whites
- 3 tablespoons water
- ¾ cup panko breadcrumbs
- ½ cup grated Parmesan cheese
- ¾ teaspoon crushed dried rosemary
- 2 teaspoons garlic powder, divided
- ¼ teaspoon salt
- ¼ teaspoon ground pepper
- ½ cup mayonnaise
- ¼ cup buttermilk
- 1 teaspoon dried chives
- 1 teaspoon dried dill

Directions:
1. Preheat oven to 425°F. Place a wire rack on a large rimmed baking sheet; coat with cooking spray. If using whole portobellos, twist off and discard stems; use a spoon to scrape off the brown gills from the undersides of the caps. Slice the caps 1/2 inch thick.
2. Spread flour in a shallow dish. Lightly whisk egg whites and water in another shallow dish. Combine panko, Parmesan, rosemary, 1 teaspoon garlic powder, salt and pepper in a third shallow dish.
3. Dredge the mushroom slices in the flour, shaking off excess. Next, dredge in the egg white mixture. Finally, dredge in the panko mixture. Transfer to the prepared rack. Coat on all sides with cooking spray. Bake until browned and crispy, 15 to 18 minutes.
4. Meanwhile, combine mayonnaise, buttermilk, chives, dill and the remaining 1 teaspoon garlic
5. powder in a bowl. Serve the sauce with the mushrooms.

Nutrition facts:
Calories Per Serving 280; Total Fat: 17g; Sodium:407 mg; Total Carbs: 25g; Fiber: 5g; Sugars: 3g; Protein: 8g

Air-fryer Potato Chips

Servings: 6
Cooking Time: 15 Minutes

Ingredients:
- 2 large potatoes
- Olive oil-flavored cooking spray
- 1/2 teaspoon sea salt
- Minced fresh parsley, optional

Directions:
1. Preheat air fryer to 360°. Using a mandoline or vegetable peeler, cut potatoes into very thin slices. Transfer to a large bowl; add enough ice water to cover. Soak for 15 minutes; drain. Add more ice water and soak another 15 minutes.
2. Drain potatoes; place on towels and pat dry. Spritz potatoes with cooking spray; sprinkle with salt. In batches, place potato slices in a single layer on greased tray in air-fryer basket. Cook until crisp and golden brown, 15-17 minutes, stirring and turning every 5-7 minutes. If desired, sprinkle with parsley.

Nutrition facts:
Calories Per Serving 85; Total Fat: 0.1g; Sodium: 163mg; Total Carbs: 19.3g; Fiber: 3g; Sugars: 1.4g; Protein: 2.1g

Air Fryer Zucchini Fries - Keto

Servings: 6
Cooking Time: 20 Minutes

Ingredients:
- For the Zucchini Fries:
- 2 medium Zucchini cut into fries
- ½ cup almond flour
- ¼ cup ground pork rinds, plain
- ¼ cup grated parmesan cheese
- 1 teaspoon garlic sea salt
- 1 teaspoon dried parsley
- 1 teaspoon dried basil
- ½ teaspoon oregano
- 2 eggs, beaten
- For the sauce
- ½ cup mayonnaise
- 2 teaspoons prepared horseradish
- 2 tablespoons ketchup (no sugar added)
- 1 teaspoon smoked paprika
- 1 teaspoon garlic salt
- ½ teaspoon fresh lemon juice

Directions:
1. If you are baking them in the air fryer oven, If you are baking them in a conventional oven, preheat to 400F.
2. Set up your breading station. Mix all the almond flour, cheese, pork rinds, oregano, parsley, garlic salt and basil together in a bowl. Beat eggs together in a separate bowl.
3. Dip the zucchini into the egg, then into the breading mixture (lightly, do not press into the mixture). Shake off any excess breading and place on a baking rack (or a parchment or Silpat lined baking pan) sprayed with olive oil spray.
4. Once all the zucchini have been breaded and are on the baking racks, spray the tops with olive oil spray and bake at 400F for 15-20 minutes or until golden brown. Rotate/swap the pans half way through cooking.
5. While the zucchini fries are baking, prepare the dipping sauce. Mix all the sauce ingredients in a bowl and whisk together until combined and set aside.
6. Allow the zucchini fries to cool slightly before serving and enjoy!

Nutrition facts:
Calories Per Serving 257; Total Fat: 22g; Sodium: 730mg; Total Carbs: 5g; Fiber: 2g; Sugars: 1g; Protein: 7.3g

Cinnamon-sugar Roasted Chickpeas

Servings: 4

Ingredients:
- 1 (15 ounce) can chickpeas, rinsed
- 1 tablespoon sugar
- 1 teaspoon ground cinnamon
- ⅛ teaspoon ground pepper
- 1 tablespoon avocado oil

Directions:
1. Position rack in the upper third of oven; preheat to 450 degrees F.

2. Blot chickpeas dry. Spread on a rimmed baking sheet. Bake for 10 minutes. Meanwhile mix sugar, cinnamon and pepper in a small bowl.
3. Transfer the chickpeas to a medium bowl and toss with oil and the cinnamon-sugar mixture. Return to the baking sheet and bake, stirring once, until browned and crunchy, 15 to 20 minutes more. Let cool on the baking sheet for 15 minutes.

Nutrition facts:
Calories Per Serving125; Total Fat:5 g; Sodium: 48mg; Total Carbs: 16g; Fiber: 4g; Sugars: 3g; Protein:5 g

Air-fryer Plantains

Servings:4

Ingredients:
- 2 medium ripe plantains (about 1 1/4 pounds total), peeled and sliced (1/2-inch)
- 2 tablespoons avocado oil, divided
- ¼ teaspoon salt

Directions:
1. Preheat air fryer to 360°F for 10 minutes. Generously coat the fryer basket with cooking spray. Toss plantains with 1 tablespoon oil in a medium bowl. Working in batches if necessary, arrange the plantains in a single layer in the fryer basket. Cook for 5 minutes; flip the plantains and continue to cook until crispy and well browned, 6 to 8 minutes more. Carefully transfer plantains to a cutting board.
2. Using the flat bottom of a small bowl or skillet, smash each plantain slice into a flat disk (about 1/4-inch thick); transfer to a medium bowl. Toss the smashed plantains with the remaining 1 tablespoon oil. Working in batches if necessary, return the plantains to the fryer basket, arranging in a single layer. Cook until crisp in spots, 5 to 7 minutes. Sprinkle with salt and serve immediately.

Nutrition facts:
Calories Per Serving171; Total Fat:7 g; Sodium: 149mg; Total Carbs: 29g; Fiber: 2g; Sugars: 13g; Protein: 1g

BREAKFAST RECIPES

Easy Egg Salad

Servings: 6
Cooking Time: 20 Minutes

Ingredients:
- 1/4 cup light mayonnaise
- 1 tsp Dijon Mustard
- 1/4 tsp ground black pepper
- 1 stalks celery (diced)
- 6 large hard-boiled eggs

Directions:
1. Cut hard boiled eggs in half and remove three of the yolks from the 6 eggs (you should end up with 6 egg whites and 3 egg yolks total). Add to a medium bowl and lightly mash with a fork.
2. Add the remaining ingredients and stir to combine.
3. Store in an airtight container in the refrigerator for up to one week.

Nutrition facts:
Calories Per Serving 70; Total Fat: 4.5g; Sodium: 150mg; Total Carbs: 2g; Fiber: 0g; Sugars: 1g; Protein: 5g

Fast-fix Bean Burrito

Servings: 1
Cooking Time: 1 Minutes

Ingredients:
- 1 8-inch whole-wheat flour tortilla
- 1/4 cup vegetarian refried beans
- 1/3 cup prepared guacamole or mashed avocado
- 1/2 cup mixed salad greens
- 1/4 cup pico de gallo or jarred salsa

Directions:
1. Place the tortilla on a microwave-safe plate. Using a spatula, spread the beans onto the tortilla, leaving about a 1-inch rim.
2. Heat in the microwave on high for 20 seconds, or until warm. Top with the guacamole, salad greens, and pico de gallo. Roll up or fold the tortilla over the fillings and serve.

Nutrition facts:
Calories Per Serving 340; Total Fat: 15g; Sodium: 410mg; Total Carbs: 45g; Fiber: 12g; Sugars: 4g; Protein: 11g

Herbed Soft Scrambled Eggs On Toast

Servings: 2
Cooking Time: 5 Minutes

Ingredients:
- 2 slices sprouted whole-grain or whole-wheat bread
- 1 tsp olive oil
- 2 eggs
- 1/8 tsp salt
- 1/4 cup loosely packed chopped fresh herbs

Directions:
1. Toast the bread in a toaster or toaster oven to desired doneness.
2. While the bread is toasting, prepare the eggs: fully heat the oil in a medium stick-resistant skillet over medium-low heat. Pour the eggs into the hot skillet and cook while gently stirring (or folding) the mixture until the eggs are no longer runny, yet are still moist, about 1 1/2–2 minutes. Remove the skillet from the heat, sprinkle with the salt, and gently stir (or fold) in the herbs.
3. Transfer the toasts to plates. Top each toast with half the herbed eggs. If desired, sprinkle with freshly ground black pepper to taste. Serve.

Nutrition facts:
Calories Per Serving 170; Total Fat: 8g; Sodium: 290mg; Total Carbs: 16g; Fiber: 3g; Sugars: 0g; Protein: 11g

Cinnamon French Vanilla Overnight Oats

Servings: 2

Ingredients:
- 1 cup quick cooking oats
- 1 tsp chia seeds
- 1/2 tsp ground cinnamon
- 1 (8-oz) bottle Splenda Diabetes Care Vanilla Shake
- 1/2 tsp vanilla extract
- 1 apple (sliced)

Directions:
1. In a small bowl, combine oats, chia seeds, and cinnamon.
2. Add Splenda Diabetes Care Vanilla Shake and vanilla extract to oat mixture. Stir until combined.
3. Divide the oat mixture evenly between two containers with lids. Cover and place in the refrigerator overnight.
4. Top each container with half the apple slices before serving.

Nutrition facts:
Calories Per Serving 290; Total Fat: 8g; Sodium: 95mg; Total Carbs: 47g; Fiber: 10g; Sugars: 9g; Protein: 14g

Guilt-free Breakfast Sausage Patties

Servings: 14
Cooking Time: 10 Minutes

Ingredients:
- 2 lbs lean ground turkey
- 1 tsp poultry seasoning
- 1 tsp fennel seeds
- 1/2 tsp onion powder
- 1 tbsp fresh parsley (chopped)
- 1/4 tsp crushed red pepper flakes (optional)
- 1/2 tsp salt
- 1/4 tsp black pepper
- 1 tbsp maple syrup

Directions:
1. Combine all ingredients in a large bowl and mix well. Shape mixture into 28 (2-inch) patties
2. In a large skillet over medium-low heat, cook patties 3-5 minutes per side, or until no longer pink in center. Serve immediately.

Nutrition facts:
Calories Per Serving 100; Total Fat: 4.5g; Sodium: 130mg; Total Carbs: 1g; Fiber: 0g; Sugars: 1g; Protein: 12g

Breakfast Quesadilla

Servings: 6
Cooking Time: 16 Minutes

Ingredients:
- 1 nonstick cooking spray
- 1/4 cup canned green chiles
- 4 eggs (beaten)
- 1/4 tsp black pepper
- 2 10-inch whole wheat flour tortillas
- 1 1/2 cup reduced fat cheddar cheese, or use Mexican blend, Monterey Jack, or pepper jack (reduced fat)
- 4 slice turkey bacon (cooked crisp and crumbled)

Directions:
1. Coat a small skillet lightly with cooking spray.
2. Saute green chiles over medium-low heat for 1-2 minutes. Add beaten eggs and cook, stirring, until scrambled and set. Season with pepper.
3. Coat a second, large skillet lightly with cooking spray. Place one tortilla in the skillet and cook over medium heat until air bubbles begin to form, about 1 minute. Flip tortilla over and cook for 1 minutes more (do not let tortilla get crispy).
4. Spread half the cheese evenly over the tortilla, covering to the edges.
5. Reduce heat to low. Quickly arrange half the cooked bacon and half the egg mixture over the cheese. Cook until the cheese starts to melt, about 1 minute.
6. Fold tortilla in half to create a half-moon shape. Flip folded tortilla over and cook until it is lightly toasted and the cheese filling is completely melted, 1-2 minutes.
7. Transfer quesadilla to a cutting board. Recoat the skillet with cooking spray, and repeat with the second tortilla and remaining cheese, bacon, and egg mixture.

8. Cut each quesadilla into 3 wedges and serve immediately with fresh salsa.

Nutrition facts:
Calories Per Serving 160; Total Fat: 10g; Sodium: 460mg; Total Carbs: 8g; Fiber: 5g; Sugars: 1g; Protein: 14g

Spinach And Parmesan Egg Bites

Servings:8
Cooking Time: 20 Minutes

Ingredients:
- 1 nonstick cooking spray
- 10 oz frozen spinach (thawed and squeezed dry)
- 1/4 cup roasted red peppers (drained and chopped)
- 2 green onions (thinly sliced)
- 1 tbsp plus 1 tsp grated Parmesan cheese
- 1 cup egg substitute
- 1/2 cup skim milk
- 1 tsp mustard powder
- 1/8 tsp salt
- 1/8 tsp black pepper

Directions:
1. Preheat the oven to 350°F. Lightly spray 16 cups of two 12-cup mini muffin pans or 16 cups of a 24-cup mini muffin pan with cooking spray.
2. In a medium bowl, using a fork, separate the spinach into small pieces. Stir in the roasted peppers and green onions. Spoon the spinach mixture into the sprayed muffin cups. Sprinkle the Parmesan over the spinach mixture.
3. In a separate medium bowl, whisk together the remaining ingredients. Pour into the filled muffin cups. Fill the empty muffin cups with water to keep the pan from warping.
4. Bake for 18–20 minutes, or until a wooden toothpick inserted in the center comes out clean. Transfer the pans to a cooling rack. Let cool for 10 minutes. Using a thin spatula or flat knife, loosen the sides of the quiche bites. Serve warm.
5. Refrigerate leftovers in an airtight container for up to 5 days. To reheat, put 4–6 quiche bites on a microwaveable plate. Microwave on 100% power (high) for 45 seconds to 1 minute, or until heated through.

Nutrition facts:
Calories Per Serving 50; Total Fat: 1.5g; Sodium: 190mg; Total Carbs: 3g; Fiber:1g; Sugars: 1g; Protein: 6g

Oat Congee

Servings:4
Cooking Time: 15 Minutes

Ingredients:
- 1 nonstick cooking spray
- 1 tbsp lime juice
- 1 cup white (button) mushrooms (rebanado)
- 1 tbsp soy sauce (reducido en sodio)
- 4 cup low sodium vegetable broth (bajo en sodio)
- 1 cup old fashioned rolled oats
- 2 green onion (scallion) (rebanado)
- 4 eggs
- 1 tbsp cilantro (finamente picada)

Directions:
1. Add oats, broth, and soy sauce to the hot pot. Bring to a boil, then simmer over low heat until the oats soften, about 10 minutes.
2. Cover a small non stick casserole with spray oil. Add mushrooms, stir fry until soft, and let all liquids evaporate for about 4 minutes. Add lemon juice and stir fry until the liquid evaporates. He put mushrooms in Congee.
3. Clean the casserole, then add oil spray. Stir fry the eggs until the yolk is almost cooked.
4. In a bowl, pour 3/4 cup oatmeal Congee, cover with a fried egg and 1 1/2 cdita. Scallions and coriander. Repeat for the remaining 3 bowls.

Nutrition facts:
Calories Per Serving 175; Total Fat: 6g; Sodium: 355mg; Total Carbs:19g; Fiber: 3g; Sugars: 3g; Protein: 0g

Meat Lover's Breakfast Cups

Servings: 6

Ingredients:
- 1 tbsp light sour cream
- 2 precooked turkey breakfast sausage patties (thawed and diced)
- 1 clove garlic (minced)
- 2 tbsp onion(s) (finely chopped)
- 1 1/4 cup frozen hash browns (thawed)
- 1 tsp canola oil
- 1/4 tsp salt
- 1/8 tsp black pepper
- 1 cup egg substitute
- 2 tbsp turkey bacon
- 2 tbsp Monterey jack cheese

Directions:
1. Preheat the oven to 400 F. Coat a six-cup muffin tin with nonstick cooking spray. Evenly divide the hash browns among the muffin cups and press firmly into the bottom and up the sides of each cup.
2. In a large skillet, heat the oil over medium heat. Sauté the onion until tender. Add the garlic and sausage; cook for 1 minute more. Remove the skillet from the heat; stir in the sour cream.
3. In a medium bowl, beat the egg substitute with the salt and black pepper, then pour it evenly into the potato-lined muffin cups. Top each cup with some of the sausage mixture, bacon, and cheese.
4. Bake 15 to 18 minutes, or until the eggs are set. Serve immediately, or freeze for later.

Nutrition facts:
Calories Per Serving 110; Total Fat: 5g; Sodium: 340mg; Total Carbs: 9g; Fiber: 1g; Sugars: 1g; Protein: 8g

Veggie Breakfast Wrap

Servings: 2
Cooking Time: 8 Minutes

Ingredients:
- 2 tsp olive oil or other vegetable oil
- 1 cup sliced mushrooms
- 2 eggs
- 1/2 cup egg white or egg substitute
- 1 cup, firmly packed spinach or other greens
- 2 tbsp chopped scallions or other onion
- 1 nonstick cooking spray
- 2 whole wheat, low-carb flour tortillas, such as La Tortilla Factory
- 2 tbsp salsa

Directions:
1. Add olive oil to the skillet over medium heat. Add mushrooms and sauté until nicely brown at edges (about 3 minutes), set aside.
2. Beat eggs with egg whites or egg substitute in medium sized bowl, using a mixer or by hand, until blended. Stir in shredded spinach, and scallions. You could also added fresh or dried herbs such as basil or parsley for moe flavor.
3. Begin heating medium/large nonstick skillet over medium-low heat. Coat pan generously with cooking spray. Pour in egg mixture and continue to scramble the mixture as it cooks using a spatula. When eggs are cooked to your liking, turn off the heat and stir in mushrooms.
4. Spread half of the egg mixture down the center of each tortilla. top each with 1 tablespoon fresh salsa or other sauce of your choice. Garnish with additional toppings like avocado slices, bell pepper or tomato if desired, then roll it up to make a wrap.

Nutrition facts:
Calories Per Serving 210; Total Fat: 12g; Sodium: 450mg; Total Carbs: 14g; Fiber: 9g; Sugars: 2g; Protein: 20g

Instant Pot Wheat Berry, Black Bean, And Avocado Salad

Servings: 4
Cooking Time: 35 Minutes

Ingredients:
- 1/3 cup dried black beans
- 1/2 cup hard wheat berries
- 4 cup water
- 2 cup grape tomatoes
- 1 cup poblano chile pepper (chopped)
- 1/2 cup fresh cilantro (chopped)
- 2 tbsp Apple Cider Vinegar
- 2 tbsp extra virgin olive oil
- 1 clove garlic (minced)
- 1/2 tsp salt
- 1 avocado (peeled and chopped)
- 3 oz reduced fat sharp cheddar cheese (shredded)

Directions:
1. Place beans and wheat berries in a fine mesh sieve, rinse and drain. Place in pressure cooker with the 4 cups water. Lock the lid in place and close the seal valve. Press the Manual button for 25 minutes. When the cook time ends, use a quick pressure release.
2. Meanwhile, combine the tomatoes, peppers, cilantro, vinegar, oil, garlic and salt, in a large bowl and set aside.
3. When valve drops, carefully remove lid, drain in a fine mesh colander and run under cold water to cool completely. drain well. Add the wheat berry mixture, avocado and cheese to the tomato mixture; toss gently until well coated. Serve as is or over leafy greens such as kale

Nutrition facts:
Calories Per Serving 320; Total Fat: 17g; Sodium: 480mg; Total Carbs: 33g; Fiber: 9g; Sugars: 6g; Protein: 13g

Breakfast Egg And Ham Burrito

Servings: 4

Ingredients:
- 4 eggs
- 4 egg whites
- 1 Dash hot pepper sauce
- 1/4 tsp black pepper
- 2 tbsp cheddar cheese (reduced-fat, shredded)
- 2 tsp margarine (trans fat-free)
- 4 slice deli ham (reduced-sodium, chopped, (about 3 ounces))
- 1/4 cup onion(s) (diced)
- 1/4 cup green pepper (diced)
- 4 corn tortillas (heated)
- 4 tsp salsa

Directions:
1. In a medium bowl, whisk together the eggs, egg whites, hot pepper sauce, black pepper, and cheese.
2. Heat the margarine in a medium non-stick pan over medium heat. Add the ham and sauté for 2-3 minutes. Remove the ham from the pan.
3. Add the onions and green peppers to the hot pan, and cook for about 5 minutes. Add the ham back to pan.
4. Reduce the heat to low and add the eggs to pan. Gently stir the eggs with a spoon or spatula and continue lightly cooking over low heat until the eggs are cooked and set.
5. Evenly divide the egg mixture into 4 servings. Spoon each portion of the egg mixture into a tortilla and top each with 1 tsp. salsa. Fold the tortilla to close.

Nutrition facts:
Calories Per Serving 200; Total Fat: 8g; Sodium: 380mg; Total Carbs: 15g; Fiber: 2g; Sugars: 2g; Protein: 16g

Air Fryer Crisp Egg Cups

Servings:4
Cooking Time: 13 Minutes

Ingredients:
- 1 nonstick cooking spray
- 4 slice whole wheat bread (toasted)
- 1 1/2 tbsp trans-fat free tub margarine (such as I Can't Believe It's Not Butter)
- 1 slice (about 2 oz) deli style ham
- 4 large eggs
- 1/8 tsp salt
- 1/8 tsp black pepper

Directions:
1. Preheat the air fryer, with the air fryer basket in place, to 375°F.
2. Spray 4 (8-ounce) oven-proof custard cups or ramekins with nonstick cooking spray.
3. Remove the crusts from the bread and discard or save for other use. Spread one side of the bread with the margarine. Place the bread, margarine-side-down into a ramekin and press gently to shape the bread to the cup. Repeat three more times. Slice the ham into strips about 1/2-inch wide. Place the strips in a single layer in the cups. Crack one egg into each cup. Sprinkle with salt and pepper.
4. Place the filled, uncovered custard cups in the air fryer basket. Air fry for 10–13 minutes or until the eggs are softly set or done as desired. Carefully remove the ramekin from the air fryer basket. Using a hot pad, hold the cup carefully and run a knife around the sides to transfer to a plate.

Nutrition facts:
Calories Per Serving 150; Total Fat: 8g; Sodium: 410mg; Total Carbs: 6g; Fiber: 1g; Sugars: 1g; Protein: 12g

Lemon Chiffon With Fresh Berries

Servings:6
Cooking Time: 10 Minutes

Ingredients:
- 1/3 cup fresh lemon juice (strained of seeds, about 2 large lemons)
- 1/2 cup granulated Splenda
- 4 large eggs
- 3 cup fresh berries (such as strawberries, blueberries, and blackberries)

Directions:
1. Place lemon juice and Splenda in saucepan. Heat and stir until sugar dissolves. Remove from heat.
2. Crack eggs into the bowl and whisk well. Slowly pour the lemon sugar mix into the eggs while whisking. Whisk for 1 minute, then return the egg mixture to the saucepan. Whisk and cook on low to medium for several minutes until the egg mixture thickens. (The more you whisk, the lighter the mixture will be.) This will take 2-5 minutes depending on your equipment. The mixture is ready to be removed from heat when it coats the back of a spoon. Refrigerate for one hour or more. It will thicken more as it cools.
3. Place some of the lemon chiffon in a dessert glass or bowl and spoon berries over or layer lemon cream and berries. Top with berries.

Nutrition facts:
Calories Per Serving 90; Total Fat: 3.5g; Sodium: 50mg; Total Carbs: 11g; Fiber: 2g; Sugars: 7g; Protein: 5g

High-fiber Zucchini Muffins

Servings:12

Ingredients:
- 1 nonstick cooking spray
- 1 can black beans (15-ounce, rinsed and drained)
- 1/4 cup water
- 2 cup zucchini (grated, (about 1 1/2 medium zucchini))
- 2 cup baking mix (gluten-free, (such as Pamela's))
- 1/2 tsp salt

- 2 tsp ground cinnamon
- 1/4 tsp ground nutmeg
- 1 eggs
- 2 egg whites
- 1/2 cup Splenda Sugar Blend
- 3 tbsp canola oil
- 1 tsp vanilla extract
- 1 tsp Apple Cider Vinegar

Directions:
1. Preheat oven to 350 degrees. Line muffin tins with muffin papers and spray with cooking spray.
2. Place black beans and water in a food processor and blend for 2-3 minutes, until you reach pumpkin consistency. Set aside.
3. Use a paper towel to wring out excess moisture from grated zucchini, set aside.
4. In a large bowl combine baking mix, salt, cinnamon and nutmeg.
5. In another bowl, whisk together eggs, Splenda Sugar Blend, oil, vanilla and vinegar. Add black bean mixture and mix well.
6. Make a well in dry ingredients and add wet ingredients. Mix well.
7. Gently fold zucchini into muffin batter.
8. Spoon batter into 12 muffin cups.
9. Bake for 22-25 minutes or until a toothpick inserted in center comes out clean.
10. Remove from oven and let muffins cool in pan for 10 minutes. Remove muffins from pan and cool completely on a wire rack.

Nutrition facts:
Calories Per Serving 185; Total Fat: 6g; Sodium: 335mg; Total Carbs: 28g; Fiber: 3g; Sugars: 10g; Protein: 5g

Breaded Air-fryer Summer Squash

Servings:4
Cooking Time: 10 Minutes

Ingredients:
- 4 cups thinly sliced yellow summer squash (3 medium)
- 3 tablespoons olive oil
- 1/2 teaspoon salt
- 1/2 teaspoon pepper
- 1/8 teaspoon cayenne pepper
- 3/4 cup panko bread crumbs
- 3/4 cup grated Parmesan cheese

Directions:
1. Preheat air fryer to 350°. Place squash in a large bowl. Add oil and seasonings; toss to coat.
2. In a shallow bowl, mix bread crumbs and cheese. Dip squash in crumb mixture to coat both sides, patting to help coating adhere. In batches, arrange squash in a single layer on tray in air-fryer basket. Cook until squash is tender and coating is golden brown, about 10 minutes.

Nutrition facts:
Calories Per Serving: 180; Total Fat: 12.3g; Sodium: 469mg; Total Carbs: 14.8g; Fiber: 1g; Sugars: 1.3g; Protein:3.5g

Crispy Air Fryer French Toast

Servings:4
Cooking Time: 6 Minutes

Ingredients:
- 2 eggs, beaten
- 2/3 cup dairy or non-dairy milk (soy or oat)
- 1 teaspoon vanilla extract
- 3/4 teaspoon cinnamon
- 12 slices French or Italian bread
- 4 tablespoons maple syrup
- 1 cup fresh blueberries, strawberries, or raspberries

Directions:
1. If your air fryer needs to be preheated, start the preheat process, aiming for 350 degrees. Lightly grease your airy fry rack so that the toast doesn't stick to it.
2. Place the eggs, milk, vanilla and cinnamon in a large plate, platter or even pie dish. Mix well with a whisk or fork until its combined.
3. Dip your bread into the mixture, letting it sit for 5-10 seconds before flipping and soaking the other side. Let any extra batter drip off each piece before placing it on the prepared rack.
4. Air fry the French toast for 3 minutes at 350 degrees. Flip the pieces and cook for another 2-3 minutes on the other side. Depending on how big

your air fryer is, you may need to do this in two batches.
5. Top your French toast with maple syrup and fresh berries.

Nutrition facts:
Calories Per Serving: 205; Total Fat: 4.3g; Sodium: 227mg; Total Carbs: 34.7g; Fiber: 3g; Sugars: 15.7g; Protein: 7.1g

Air-fryer Wasabi Egg Salad Wraps

Servings:4

Ingredients:
- 6 large eggs
- 1 ripe avocado
- 1 tablespoon lime juice
- 2 teaspoons wasabi sauce
- ¼ teaspoon salt
- ¼ teaspoon ground pepper
- ½ cup chopped cucumber
- 8 butterhead lettuce leaves
- Chopped fresh cilantro for garnish
- Lime wedges for serving

Directions:
1. Preheat air fryer to 250°F for 5 minutes. Place eggs in the air-fryer basket; cook for 20 minutes. Immediately plunge the eggs into an ice bath. Let stand until cool, about 5 minutes. Drain, peel and coarsely chop the eggs.
2. Scoop avocado flesh into a medium bowl. Add lime juice and wasabi sauce to taste; mash until mostly smooth. Stir in salt and pepper. Fold in the chopped eggs and cucumber. Divide the mixture between lettuce leaves. If desired, sprinkle with cilantro and serve with lime wedges.

Nutrition facts:
Calories Per Serving188; Total Fat: 13g; Sodium: 426mg; Total Carbs: 9g; Fiber: 3g; Sugars: 2g; Protein:11 g

Air Fryer Cheesy Baked Eggs

Servings:2
Cooking Time: 16 Minutes

Ingredients:
- 4 large Eggs
- 2 ounces Smoked gouda, chopped
- Everything bagel seasoning
- Kosher salt and pepper to taste

Directions:
1. Spray the inside of each ramekin with cooking spray. Add 2 eggs to each ramekin, then add 1 ounce of chopped gouda to each. Salt and pepper to taste. Sprinkle your everything bagel seasoning on top of each ramekin (as much as you like).
2. Place each ramekin into the air fryer basket. Cook for 400F for 16 minutes, or until eggs are cooked through. Serve.

Nutrition facts:
Calories Per Serving: 240; Total Fat: 16g; Sodium: 0mg; Total Carbs: 1g; Fiber: 0g; Sugars: 0g; Protein:12g

Air Fryer Scrambled Eggs

Servings:2
Cooking Time: 9 Minutes

Ingredients:
- 1/3 tablespoon unsalted butter
- 2 eggs
- 2 tablespoons milk
- salt and pepper to taste
- 1/8 cup cheddar cheese

Directions:
1. Place butter in an oven/air fryer-safe pan and place inside the air fryer.
2. Cook at 300 degrees until butter is melted, about 2 minutes.
3. Whisk together the eggs and milk, then add salt and pepper to taste.
4. Place eggs in pan and cook it on 300 degrees for 3 minutes, then push eggs to the inside of the pan to stir them around.
5. Cook for 2 more minutes then add cheddar cheese, stirring the eggs again.

6. Cook 2 more minutes.
7. Remove pan from the air fryer and enjoy them immediately.

Nutrition facts:
Calories Per Serving: 126; Total Fat: 9g; Sodium: 275mg; Total Carbs: 1g; Fiber: 0g; Sugars: 0g; Protein: 9g

Bangers And Mash

Servings: 6
Cooking Time: 45 Minutes

Ingredients:
- 1 nonstick cooking spray
- 2 lbs sweet potatoes (washed and dried)
- 1 whole wheat bread (crusts removed)
- 1/4 cup egg substitute
- 20 oz lean ground turkey ((93% fat-free))
- 1/2 tsp ground thyme
- 1/2 tsp ground sage
- 1 tsp garlic powder
- 1/4 tsp cayenne pepper
- 3/4 tsp salt (divided use)
- 1/2 tsp black pepper (divided use)
- 1 tbsp olive oil

Directions:
1. Preheat oven to 375 degrees F. Coat a baking sheet with cooking spray.
2. Line the sweet potatoes on the baking sheet and bake for 45 minutes or until tender when pierced with a fork. Set aside to cool slightly.
3. While the sweet potatoes are cooling, mix the whole wheat bread and egg, and mix well until bread is softened and a paste forms. Stir in the ground turkey, thyme, sage, garlic powder, cayenne pepper, 1/2 tsp of the salt, and 1/4 tsp of the black pepper.
4. Divide the sausage mixture into 6 equal sized patties and sauté in a medium non-stick sauté pan coated with cooking spray for about 4-5 minutes on each side or until the center of the patty reaches an internal temperature of 165 degrees.
5. Once the sweet potatoes have cooled slightly, peel the skins off (they should be easy to peel off by hand) and add the peeled sweet potatoes to a bowl with 1 tbsp olive oil, remaining 1/4 tsp salt, and remaining 1/4 tsp pepper. Mash with a potato masher or sturdy whisk until fluffy.
6. Serve one sausage patty on top of a scoop of the mashed sweet potatoes.

Nutrition facts:
Calories Per Serving 280; Total Fat: 10g; Sodium: 430mg; Total Carbs: 25g; Fiber: 4g; Sugars: 7g; Protein: 22g

Perfect & Easy To Peel Air Fryer Hard Boiled Eggs

Servings: 3
Cooking Time: 18 Minutes

Ingredients:
- 3 large eggs or many eggs you want
- 1 bowl filled with water and ice

Directions:
1. Place the eggs in the basket of the air fryer in a single layer.
2. Set the air fryer to cook at 280°F for 18 minutes.
3. When the cooking time is up, immediately, place the cooked eggs in the bowl of ice water to cool.
4. When eggs are cool, remove the shells before eating or store them in the fridge before peeling the shell off.

Nutrition facts:
Calories Per Serving: 95; Total Fat: 6g; Sodium: 101mg; Total Carbs: 0g; Fiber: 0g; Sugars: 0g; Protein: 8g

Brown Rice Congee With Stir-fried Herbs

Servings: 6

Ingredients:
- 2 quarts filtered water
- 1 cup brown sushi rice
- 1 tbsp grapeseed or vegetable oil
- 2 oz fresh ginger (peeled and finely julienned)
- 2 green onion (scallion) (trimmed and julienned into 1-inch-long pieces)
- 2 red Thai chilies (stems and seeds removed, thinly sliced into rounds)

- 1/2 bunch cilantro (stems trimmed and coarsely chopped (about 1 cup))

Directions:
1. Fill a large pot with the water. Add the rice, cover, and bring to a boil over high heat. Reduce heat to medium, and continue to cook until the rice grains break down and the soup thickens, about 1 hour.
2. Meanwhile in a small skillet over high heat, add the oil and stir-fry the ginger, scallions, and chilies until fragrant and lightly golden, 30-45 seconds. Add the cilantro and continue to stir-fry until just wilted, about 30 seconds more. Transfer to bowl.
3. Ladle some congee into 6 individual bowls, and top each with about 1 Tbsp. of stir-fried herbs. Mix the herbs into the porridge to distribute the flavors. Serve.

Nutrition facts:
Calories Per Serving 150; Total Fat: 3.5g; Sodium: 20mg; Total Carbs: 27g; Fiber: 2g; Protein:3g

Prosciutto And Spinach Egg Cups

Servings:6
Cooking Time: 12 Minutes

Ingredients:
- 6 slices prosciutto
- 6 eggs
- 1/2 cup baby spinach
- 1/4 teaspoons pepper , salt optional

Directions:
1. Air Fryer Egg Cups
2. Preheat your air fryer or oven to 375°F (190°C).
3. Spray or drizzle the muffin tin with oil. Lay one piece of prosciutto inside each cup, pressing to line the bottom and sides of each cup.
4. Gently press about 4-5 spinach leaves into the bottom of each cup.
5. Crack one egg into each cup. Sprinkle with a little pepper and they're ready to go into the oven or air fryer.
6. Bake in the Air Fryer. Carefully transfer your muffin tin or muffin cups to the air fryer (leave a little space between them), and close. Cook for 10 minutes.
7. Bake in Oven: If using silicone muffin cups, set them on a baking sheet. Set the muffin tin or baking sheet on the middle rack and cook for ~15 minutes for a medium cooked egg.
8. Remove the muffin tin from the oven and allow it to cool slightly, until you're able to handle it. Carefully remove each egg cup from the muffin tin.
9. Serve right away or allow to cool completely, then transfer to an airtight container and store in the refrigerator 3-4 days.

Nutrition facts:
Calories Per Serving: 97; Total Fat: 7g; Sodium: 214mg; Total Carbs: 1g; Fiber: 1g; Sugars: 1g; Protein: 7g

Printed in Great Britain
by Amazon